HOME REPAIR AND IMPROVEMENT

NEW LIVING SPACES

Other Publications
VOICES OF THE CIVIL WAR
THE TIME-LIFE COMPLETE GARDENER
JOURNEY THROUGH THE MIND AND BODY
WEIGHT WATCHERS® SMART CHOICE RECIPE COLLECTION
TRUE CRIME
THE AMERICAN INDIANS
THE ART OF WOODWORKING
LOST CIVILIZATIONS
ECHOES OF GLORY
THE NEW FACE OF WAR
HOW THINGS WORK
WINGS OF WAR
CREATIVE EVERYDAY COOKING
COLLECTOR'S LIBRARY OF THE UNKNOWN
CLASSICS OF WORLD WAR II
TIME-LIFE LIBRARY OF CURIOUS AND UNUSUAL FACTS
AMERICAN COUNTRY
VOYAGE THROUGH THE UNIVERSE
THE THIRD REICH
MYSTERIES OF THE UNKNOWN
TIME FRAME
FIX IT YOURSELF
FITNESS, HEALTH AND NUTRITION
SUCCESSFUL PARENTING
HEALTHY HOME COOKING
UNDERSTANDING COMPUTERS
LIBRARY OF NATIONS
THE ENCHANTED WORLD
THE KODAK LIBRARY OF CREATIVE PHOTOGRAPHY
GREAT MEALS IN MINUTES
THE CIVIL WAR
PLANET EARTH
COLLECTOR'S LIBRARY OF THE CIVIL WAR
THE EPIC OF FLIGHT
THE GOOD COOK
WORLD WAR II
THE OLD WEST

*For information on and a full description
of any of the Time-Life Books series listed above,
please call 1-800-621-7026 or write:*
Reader Information
Time-Life Customer Service
P.O. Box C-32068
Richmond, Virginia 23261-2068

HOME REPAIR AND IMPROVEMENT

NEW LIVING SPACES

BY THE EDITORS OF TIME-LIFE BOOKS, ALEXANDRIA, VIRGINIA

The Consultants
Jeff Palumbo is a registered journeyman carpenter
who has a home-building and remodeling business
in northern Virginia. His interest in carpentry was
sparked by his grandfather, a master carpenter with
more than 50 years' experience. Mr. Palumbo teaches
in the Fairfax County Adult Education Program.

Mark M. Steele is a professional home inspector in
the Washington, D.C., area. He has developed and
conducted training programs in home-ownership skills
for first-time homeowners. He appears frequently on
television and radio as an expert in home repair and
consumer topics.

CONTENTS

Easy Transformations

1

Most houses contain a surprising amount of space that can be altered or adapted to fit your family's needs. This chapter shows how you can use prefabricated items for the purpose. A large accordion door—or another type of door in an opening between rooms—can create two private spaces or conceal a work area. You can even expand living space outward with readymades, adding a patio cover to make an outdoor area far more useful.

An Accordion Door to Divide a Room

Accordion folding doors, named for the bellows of the instrument they resemble, can be purchased large enough to span the entire width of a room. Riding easily on rollers in a ceiling track, an accordion door can be closed to make two rooms from one, yet it folds compactly to one side when open. Accordion doors are available at most home centers, but one large enough to partition a room may need to be custom-ordered.

A Suspended Header: At 6 feet 8 inches, most accordion doors are too short for the typical 8-foot ceiling. Installation, therefore, usually involves adding a header to lower the ceiling at the door location.

The header is constructed as shown on the next page. Hanging procedures vary depending on whether the ceiling covering (wallboard, for example) is attached directly to overhead joists *(page 10)* or suspended below them *(pages 11-12)*. Many floors have a slight slope; to avoid having the door bind, the header should be installed parallel to the floor, rather than perfectly level.

Header Dimensions: Measure from floor to ceiling at several points along the proposed line of the door. Subtract from the shortest of these measurements the height of the door, as well as the thickness of its track and the wallboard to be applied to the header. The result is the height of the header frame. Its length is the distance from wall to wall.

 TOOLS

Electronic stud finder
Chalk line
Hammer
Plumb bob
Circular saw
Carpenter's level
Electric drill with
   wood bit ($\frac{9}{16}$")
   and spade bit (1")
Utility knife

 MATERIALS

2 x 4s
Common nails ($3\frac{1}{2}$")
Screws ($1\frac{1}{2}$")
Perforated metal
   strapping
Cedar shims
Lag screws ($\frac{1}{2}$" x $3\frac{1}{2}$")
   and washers
Threaded metal rods
   ($\frac{1}{2}$"), nuts, and
   washers
Wood screws or
   hollow-wall anchors

 **SAFETY TIPS**

Earplugs provide important protection when you are hammering for long periods or operating a circular saw. Wear goggles when hammering overhead or operating a circular saw.

POSITIONING THE DOOR

1. Locating the joists.

Use an electronic stud finder to pinpoint joists behind the ceiling where you plan to install your accordion door. If the door will cross the room perpendicular to the joists, pencil a mark at the center of each one.

For a door running the other direction, you will need to install blocking between two ceiling joists as shown for a suspended ceiling on page 12. Find the two joists nearest the door location and mark their centers near both ends. (For a door directly below a joist, plan to install the header flush with one side of the joist.)

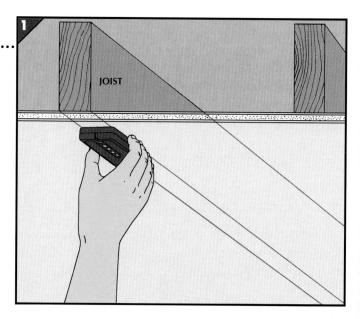

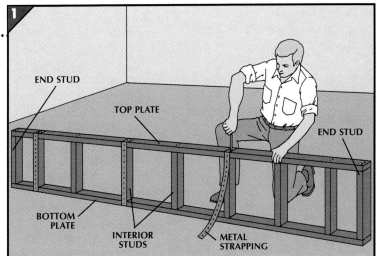

2. Marking for the header.

Where practical, plan to install the header so that it aligns with studs in the walls. Otherwise you must install nailer blocks between the studs *(page 26, Step 3).*

◆ Snap a chalk line across the ceiling to mark the location for the centerline of the header. In the illustration at right, the chalk line has been wrapped around nails hammered partway into the corners formed by the walls and ceiling.

◆ On the wall to which you plan to anchor the accordion door, suspend the chalk line from the nail and snap a vertical line all the way to the floor. On the opposite wall, extend a similar line from the nail to a point just below where the base of the header will be; this avoids marring the wall finish. The wall lines serve as guides for installing the door's overhead track and wall panel *(pages 13-14).*

HANGING A HEADER

1. Making the header.

◆ From 2-by-4s, cut a top plate and a bottom plate the width of the room. Also cut two end studs to the height of the frame minus 3 inches.

◆ Fasten the two studs to the ends of the top and bottom plates with $3\frac{1}{2}$-inch nails, forming a rectangle.

◆ Fill in the rectangle with additional studs spaced 16 inches apart and nailed in place through the plates. If the header is to run across the joists, set the first of these interior studs 8 inches from one of the end studs and 16 inches apart thereafter. Doing so offsets them from the joists, to which you will later nail the header.

◆ Reinforce the frame at every other stud with perforated metal strapping fastened with $1\frac{1}{2}$-inch screws. Cut the straps to fit over the top plate, down the stud, and across the bottom plate as shown here.

A Convenient Nail-Pouch Accessory

A pouch that attaches to your belt is a handy place to keep nails or screws as you build wood framing. Reaching into the supply of fasteners can be painful, however, because of their sharp points. One alternative is to slit the belt loop of the pouch for rubber bands to hold a magnet *(photograph).* You can then pull fasteners off the magnet as needed; because they are visible and also somewhat more separated, you are less likely to be annoyed by small cuts.

2. Attaching the header.

With a helper, hold the frame against the ceiling, centered on the lines chalked on the walls in Step 2 on page 9, and fasten the end studs to the walls with nails hammered partway into studs or nailer blocks you've installed *(above)*.

3. Shimming the frame.

◆ At several points along the header, measure from the header to the floor.

◆ To make these distances uniform, insert wood shims as needed between top plate and ceiling. A good technique is to push in shims from opposite sides of the top plate to form a tight rectangular block *(right)*.

◆ Seat the end-stud nails into the wall.

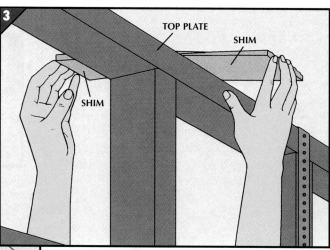

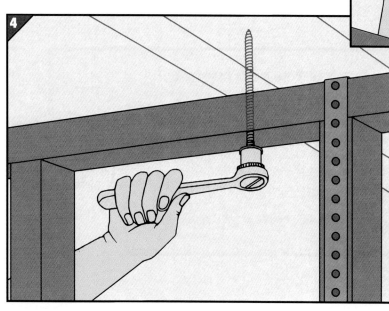

4. Securing the frame.

◆ Nail the top plate of the frame to the joists or nailer blocks.

◆ For extra security, fasten the frame to every other joist or nailer block with $\frac{1}{2}$- by $3\frac{1}{2}$-inch lag screws and washers *(left)*.

◆ Score protruding shims flush with the top plate, then snap off the ends.

◆ Finish the frame with wallboard *(pages 36-42)*.

1. Preparing the support and header.

◆ Remove ceiling panels and cross Ts from the ceiling framework along the line proposed for the door, then cut three 2-by-4s long enough to span the room—two for the header frame and one for a support above the ceiling.

◆ Hold one of the boards in position against the joists and mark it every 2 feet or so, but only where you can insert a $\frac{1}{2}$-inch-diameter threaded rod without encountering joists, pipes, ducts, or the ceiling framework (above).

◆ Stack the marked 2-by-4 on one of the others and drill $\frac{9}{16}$-inch holes for the rods through both.

2. Installing the support and header.

◆ With $3\frac{1}{2}$-inch nails, attach one of the drilled 2-by-4s to the joists as a header support. Secure the support to every other joist with a $\frac{1}{2}$- by $3\frac{1}{2}$-inch lag screw and washer.

◆ For each hole in the support, cut a $\frac{1}{2}$-inch threaded rod 3 inches longer than the distance from the top of the support to the ceiling framework.

◆ Insert a rod through each hole, sandwiching it between two nuts and washers. Let the rods protrude about 2 inches below the ceiling framework.

◆ Use the other drilled board as the top plate of a header that is constructed as shown on page 9.

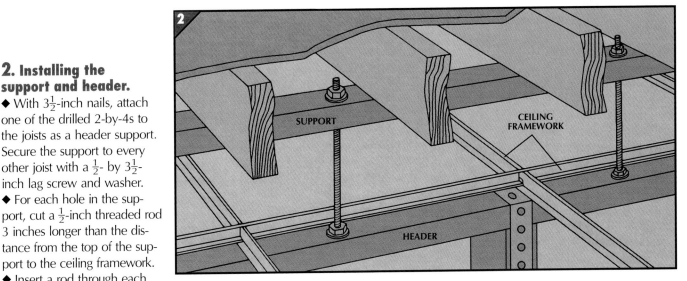

◆ Connect the header to the rods with a nut and washer above and below the top plate. Set the header at a uniform distance from the floor by adjusting the nuts at the support.

3. Trimming and replacing ceiling panels.

◆ As you reinstall the ceiling panels removed earlier, mark the edge of each one where it meets a supporting rod.

◆ For rods near panel edges, simply notch the panel with a utility knife, then fit the panel around the rod.

◆ If the supporting rods meet ceiling panels nearer the center, cut each panel in two where the edge meets the rod.

◆ Notch both sides of the cut to accommodate the rods and fit the two ceiling-panel pieces into position.

A SUSPENDED-CEILING HEADER PARALLEL TO JOISTS

1. Installing supports.

Proceed as follows to hang a header between joists above a suspended ceiling. If the header is directly below a joist, place the blocking between that joist and a neighbor.

◆ Cut lengths of 2-by-4 to fit between adjacent joists at intervals of about 2 feet.

◆ For joists made of ordinary lumber as shown in the large illustration at right, secure the 2-by-4 support blocks with $3\frac{1}{2}$-inch nails, flush with the bottoms of the joists.

◆ Snap a chalk line across the supports between the wall lines marked in Step 2 on page 9. With a $\frac{9}{16}$-inch bit, drill a hole on the chalked mark through each support, centering the hole between the edges of the support.

◆ Cut threaded rods and install them in the supports (page 11, Step 2).

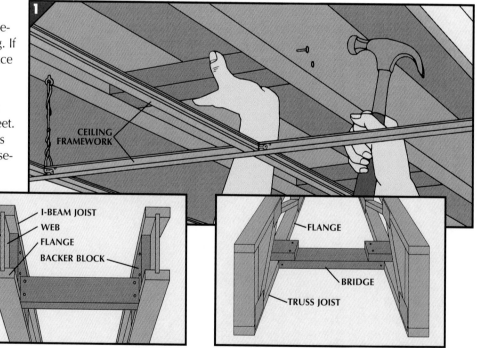

For I-beam joists (left inset), nail wood backer blocks in place beside the webbing, flush with the flange edges; angle the nails slightly so they reach the flanges. Then turn the blocking supports on edge; toenail the top of the support to the block

and the bottom to the lower flange. Drill the holes for threaded rods with an extra-long bit.

Truss joists require a bridge constructed as shown in the right inset. After setting the bridge in place, toenail it to the joist flanges.

2. Attaching the header.

◆ Cut two 2-by-4s long enough to span the room at the door's planned location.
◆ With a helper, hold one of the boards against the rods and tap it gently to mark their locations.
◆ Drill $\frac{9}{16}$-inch holes at the marks.
◆ Construct a header *(page 9, Step 1)*, using this board as the top plate and the other 2-by-4 as the bottom plate.
◆ Connect the header to the rods and adjust it so that it parallels the slope of the floor *(page 11, Step 2)*.

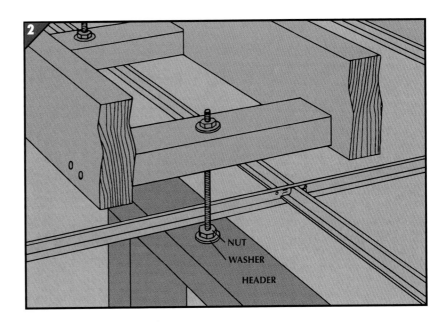

NUT
WASHER
HEADER

ATTACHING THE DOOR

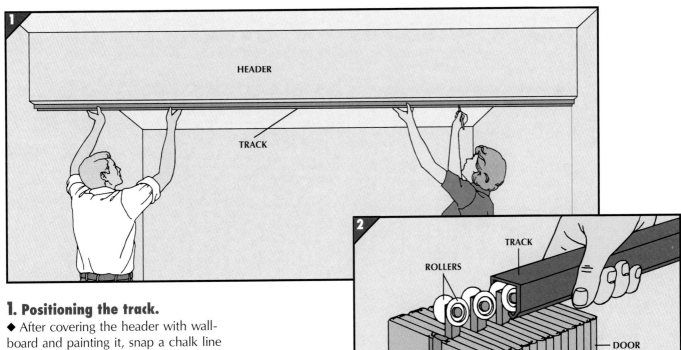

HEADER

TRACK

TRACK

ROLLERS

DOOR

1. Positioning the track.

◆ After covering the header with wall-board and painting it, snap a chalk line across the base of the header from one of the wall lines to the other.
◆ Hold the track against the new line and mark the screw holes *(above)*.
◆ Take down the track and drill pilot holes for the screws provided by the door manufacturer.

2. Attaching the door.

Without removing the tape or cardboard retaining bands that compress the folds of the door, slip the rollers at the top of the door into the track *(above)*.

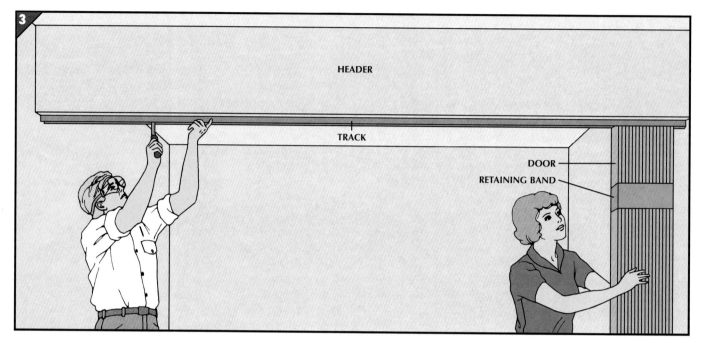

3. Mounting the door.

◆ Stand the entire assembly beneath the header with the door at one end of the track. Make sure to raise the assembly with the wall panel facing the wall with the floor-to-ceiling chalked line.

◆ Screw the other end of the track to the header *(above)*.

◆ Slide the door to the fastened end of the track and screw the rest of the track to the header.

4. Positioning the strike plate.

◆ Along the vertical line on the wall, attach the door's wall panel, which is usually a hinged half panel with holes predrilled for mounting. Use wood screws unless there is no stud behind the wall panel; in that case substitute hollow-wall anchors.

◆ Extend the door to the opposite wall.

◆ Position the strike plate to accept the latch on the door—in several models, both strike plate and door latch are magnetized—and fasten it to the wall *(right)*.

◆ Attach the door handles according to the manufacturer's instructions.

Doors for a Wall Opening

Adding doors to a wide opening between two rooms can make both spaces more useful. Doors can turn an alcove into a guest bedroom, for example, or reduce the noise from a laundry area. As shown here and on pages 16 to 18, two types of doors are commonly used for this purpose: bifold and sliding. Both are sold in kits with special mounting hardware.

A Choice of Doors: Bifold doors consist of wood, plastic, glass, or metal panels hinged together lengthwise in pairs. One or more pairs of panels can be mounted at one side of an opening and pulled all the way across; more commonly, a pair of panels is installed at each side of an opening and the pairs are brought together at the middle.

Sliding doors, which roll open at a touch, consist of two wood panels, each hung by wheels from its own overhead track. The panels overlap at the center, and when closed are kept aligned by a small floor-mounted guide. In daily use, sliding doors block half the opening. They can be lifted off the tracks, however, when you need to make use of the whole opening—to move furniture, for example.

Door Height Restrictions: Bifold and sliding doors come in many widths, but the choice of heights is quite limited. Most bifold doors are intended for an opening 6 feet 8 inches high. Sliding doors fit into an opening about 6 feet 10 inches high; the exact height depends on the hardware. Adapt sliding doors to a shorter opening by trimming the panels *(page 45)*. If an opening is too tall for either type of door, you can build a header *(pages 8-13)*.

Checking for Level: Both types of door require an overhead track. Make sure the surface to which it will be attached is level. If necessary, you can shim a track by as much as $\frac{1}{4}$ inch *(page 10)*.

 TOOLS

Hacksaw
Electric drill with
 wood bits
Screwdriver
Plumb line
Hammer

 **MATERIALS**

Bifold doors
Bifold door
 hardware kit
Sliding doors
Sliding door
 hardware kit

 **SAFETY TIPS**

Protect your eyes with safety goggles when you drill holes overhead.

HANGING BIFOLD DOORS

1. Mounting the track.

◆ Measure the width of the top of the opening and the length of the track, which should be $\frac{1}{8}$ inch shorter. If necessary, cut the track to size with a hacksaw.

◆ Center the track at the top of the opening and mark for the screw holes; set the track aside.

◆ Drill pilot holes to match the screws provided with the kit.

◆ Attach the track *(right)*.

TRACK

2. Installing the bottom bracket.

◆ From the center of the top pivot bracket (which comes attached to the track), drop a plumb line to the floor *(right)* and lightly mark the floor at the indicated point.

◆ Set the bottom pivot bracket *(photograph)* in place against the side wall of the opening, with the floor mark centered between the sides of the notched slot.

◆ Drill pilot holes for the screws provided; screw the bottom bracket to the wall and the floor.

For a two-door set, follow the same procedure on the opposite side of the opening.

TOP PIVOT BRACKET

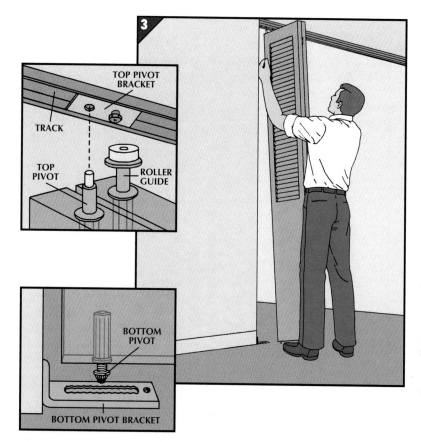

TOP PIVOT BRACKET

TRACK

TOP PIVOT

ROLLER GUIDE

BOTTOM PIVOT

BOTTOM PIVOT BRACKET

3. Preparing the door.

◆ With a hammer, gently seat the bottom pivot in the predrilled hole at the bottom of the door panel nearest the wall.

◆ Similarly insert the top pivot into the hole at the top of that door panel, and the roller guide into the hole at the top of the other panel. Both the top pivot and the roller guide are spring loaded to simplify installation.

◆ Fold the door and slip the top pivot into the top pivot bracket *(upper inset)*. Push the door upward to compress the top pivot and insert the bottom pivot into its bracket *(lower inset)*.

◆ Unfold the door, hold down the spring-mounted roller guide, and slip it into the track.

For a two-door set, install the other door the same way.

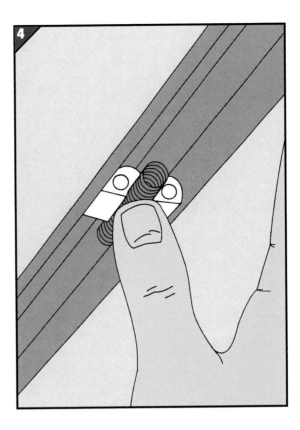

4. Securing the snugger.

Insert the snugger into the track as shown at right. For a single door, place the snugger between the roller guide and the top pivot; in the case of a two-door set, put the snugger between the doors.

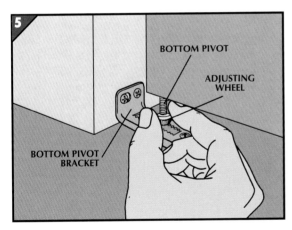

BOTTOM PIVOT

ADJUSTING WHEEL

BOTTOM PIVOT BRACKET

5. Adjusting the doors.

To raise or lower a door slightly, note which notch the bottom pivot occupies in its bracket. Then lift out the pivot and turn the adjusting wheel—counterclockwise to lower the door, clockwise to elevate it *(left)*. Reseat the pivot in the correct notch.

You can move the bottom of a door sideways by lifting the bottom pivot and moving it to another notch.

To shift the top of a door, remove the door, loosen the screw holding the top pivot bracket, and move the bracket. Retighten the screw and replace the door.

After positioning the doors, attach the handles.

6. Mounting the aligners.

Bifold doors mounted on each side of an opening and meeting in the middle when closed are usually held flush and in line with metal aligners. To install the aligners, mount one on the back of each closed door *(right)*. You can fine-tune the position of each aligner by loosening the screws and sliding the aligner along the adjustment slots.

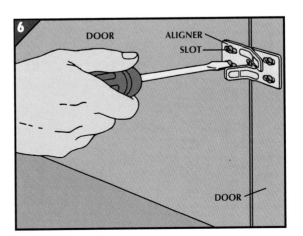

DOOR   ALIGNER
              SLOT

DOOR

PUTTING IN SLIDING DOORS

1. Hanging the doors.

◆ Order sliding doors that measure one-half the width of the opening plus $\frac{1}{2}$ inch, to allow a 1-inch overlap when the doors are closed.

◆ Fasten two wheeled carriers to the top of each door according to the manufacturer's instructions.

◆ Attach the track to the surface at the top of the opening with the open sides of the two channels toward the room that the doors will enclose.

◆ Hang the innermost door first. Facing the closed side of the track, hold the door with the top tilted away from you. Hook the carrier wheels into the rear channel (right).

◆ Hang the other door from the front channel in the same fashion.

2. Attaching the aligner assembly.

◆ Adjust the aligner assembly to the width of your sliding doors. A common design consists of a slotted metal plate and a set of plastic guides that can be inserted through different slots in the plate to accommodate doors of different widths (photograph).

◆ Hold the doors plumb and center the middle plastic guide between them. Mark the position of the aligner plate and screw holes on the floor.

◆ Drill pilot holes for the screws, then screw the aligner assembly into place (left).

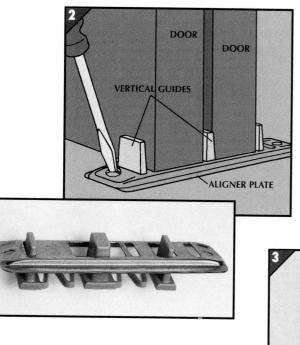

3. Aligning the doors.

To adjust the position of the doors, work from inside the room they enclose.

◆ If the edge of a door does not meet the wall squarely, loosen the adjusting screws that hold the carriers in place (inset).

◆ Push a shim between the bottom of the door and the floor until the door squares with the wall (right).

◆ Retighten the screws and remove the shim.

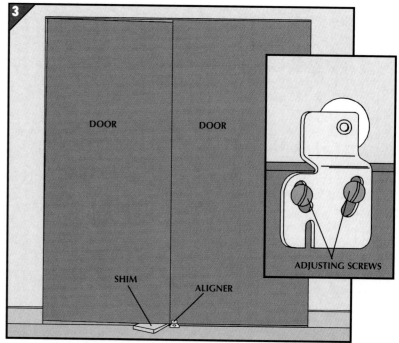

A Patio Cover for Extended Shelter

A cover of aluminum or enameled-steel roofing panels can shelter a patio or driveway next to the house from sun and rain. Precut roofing panels and frames fit together neatly, are easy to handle, and are practically maintenance free.

A Sturdy Frame: The roof consists of four channels called fascias that frame interlocking roof panels, or pans. Supported by posts on one side and attached to the house at the other, the roof is pitched away from the house to divert rainwater and snowmelt, while troughs in the end fascias act as gutters.

The procedure that appears here and on the following pages explains how to install this kind of roof over a concrete patio next to a frame house with wood, vinyl, or aluminum siding. With brick veneer, the fascia is attached with expansion bolts embedded in the mortar joints.

Getting the Right Fit: Posts to support the outer edge of the roof must be tall enough to clear the tops of doors and windows. The roof should be no larger than the patio it protects. Otherwise, you'll need to pour concrete footings to support the posts.

Patio and carport covers are available as complete packages that include all the parts and fasteners, or the components can be cut to the dimensions you specify by a building-supply dealer, who can provide matching downspouts, as well as kits to enclose the covered patio with screen or glass wall panels.

TOOLS

Stepladders
Chalk line
Electronic stud
  finder
Electric drill with bits

Carbide-tipped
  masonry bit
Caulking gun
Screwdriver
Carpenter's level

MATERIALS

Silicone caulk
Wood screws
  (3" No. 8)
Shims
2 x 4s
1 x 4

Sheet-metal
  screws (1")
Common nails
  ($2\frac{1}{2}$")
Expansion bolts
  ($\frac{1}{4}$")

SAFETY TIPS

Protect yourself from sharp-edged sheet metal by wearing goggles and work gloves. Always wear a hard hat when working under an unfinished structure and a dust mask when drilling into masonry.

---

1. Mounting the end fascia.

◆ Snap a level chalk line at support-post height on the side of the house.
◆ Check that the patio slopes away from the house. If not, raise the line to give the cover a pitch of 1 inch for every 4 feet of width. For example, if the patio extends 12 feet from the house, raise the line 3 inches.
◆ Using a stud finder *(page 8)*, mark stud centers on the line; extend the marks several inches upward.
◆ With a helper, hold one of the two end fascias against the house, its lower edge on the chalk line. At each stud mark, drill a pilot hole through the fascia and siding into the studs.
◆ Run a bead of caulk along the upper back side of the fascia; on a house built with wood siding in a region of heavy rainfall, substitute metal flashing above the fascia for caulking *(inset)*. Use the technique shown on page 90.
◆ Mount the fascia loosely to the wall with 3-inch wood

screws. On a clapboard or shingled house, insert shims behind the fascia to plumb it and then tighten the screws *(inset)*.
◆ Run another bead of caulk along the top of the fascia where it meets the siding.

2. Preparing the end and side fascias.

◆ Fit the other end fascia over the L-shaped bracket mounted at the end of a side fascia. Drill two pilot holes through the overlapping pieces for the sheet-metal screws provided in the kit, and screw the fascias together.

◆ Attach a post fitting to the underside of the end fascia approximately 1 inch from each corner, using a pair of sheet-metal screws for each fitting. If the end fascia is more than 12 feet long, mount a third post fitting midway between the corners.

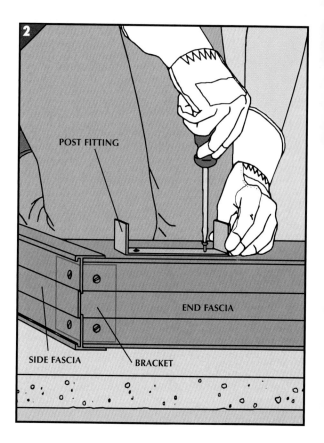

POST FITTING

END FASCIA

SIDE FASCIA

BRACKET

3. Raising the fascia frame.

◆ Make four temporary braces *(inset)* for the roof frame using 2-by-4s cut 6 inches longer than the support posts. Two inches from the end of each 2-by-4, nail a 12-inch-long crosspiece, then nail a 6-inch-long piece across that to form a U-shaped saddle.

◆ With a helper and the braces, raise the combined side and end fascia section into place. As in Step 2, secure the free end of

the side fascia to the L-shaped bracket at the end of the fascia mounted on the house.

◆ Stabilize the three-sided framework with a 1-by-4 fastened temporarily across the two

end fascias with 1-inch sheet-metal screws.

◆ Using sheet-metal screws, attach the posts to the fittings installed earlier on the underside of the fascia.

1 x 4

SIDE FASCIA

END FASCIA

TEMPORARY BRACES

20

4. Assembling the roof.

◆ Slide a roof pan into the end fascia channels at the open side of the frame, keeping the lip along the top of the pan toward you. Push the pan through the channels and secure it to the side fascia with sheet-metal screws at 12-inch intervals.

◆ Slide a second pan against the first, flexing the side of the pan to slip it under the lip of the first pan, locking the pieces together *(inset)*. Slide the remaining pans into the frame, locking each one to the preceding pan.

◆ Complete the frame by attaching the remaining piece of side fascia.

◆ Pull the last pan toward the fascia (the interlocked pans will spread sufficiently to give some play), and secure it to the fascia with sheet-metal screws.

5. Fitting the support posts.

◆ Use a carpenter's level to plumb both support posts, and pencil outlines of the bases on the slab.

◆ Align a pair of post brackets at either end of each post and mark hole positions on the slab through the predrilled hole in the bracket.

◆ Set the brackets aside and, using a carbide-tipped masonry bit in an electric drill, bore a $\frac{1}{2}$-inch-wide hole into the slab at each mark for the shield of a $\frac{1}{4}$-inch expansion bolt.

◆ Secure the brackets to the slab with the expansion bolts, then fasten the brackets to the posts with sheet-metal screws *(inset)*.

◆ Remove the temporary bracing.

◆ Working from above, fasten each pan to the end fascias with two sheet-metal screws per pan.

⚠ **CAUTION** *Do not walk on the metal roof when securing the pan ends adjacent to the house; instead lay a 4-by-8 sheet of plywood across the pans to distribute your weight.*

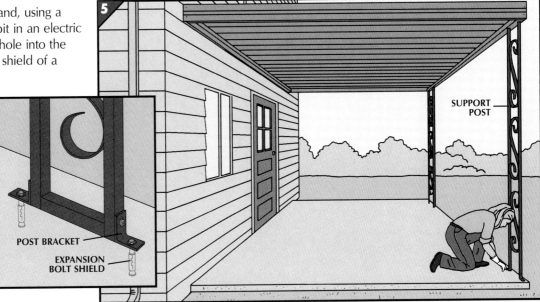

21

New and Old Walls

Nothing transforms the interior of a house more dramatically than adding new walls or taking out old ones, the two tasks explained in this chapter. As you decide which walls to add or subtract, consider the family's traffic patterns, as well as issues such as natural lighting and cross ventilation. Scale drawings can help you picture the planned alterations; for greater realism, try hanging sheets where you intend to build walls.

Finishing a wallboard joint →

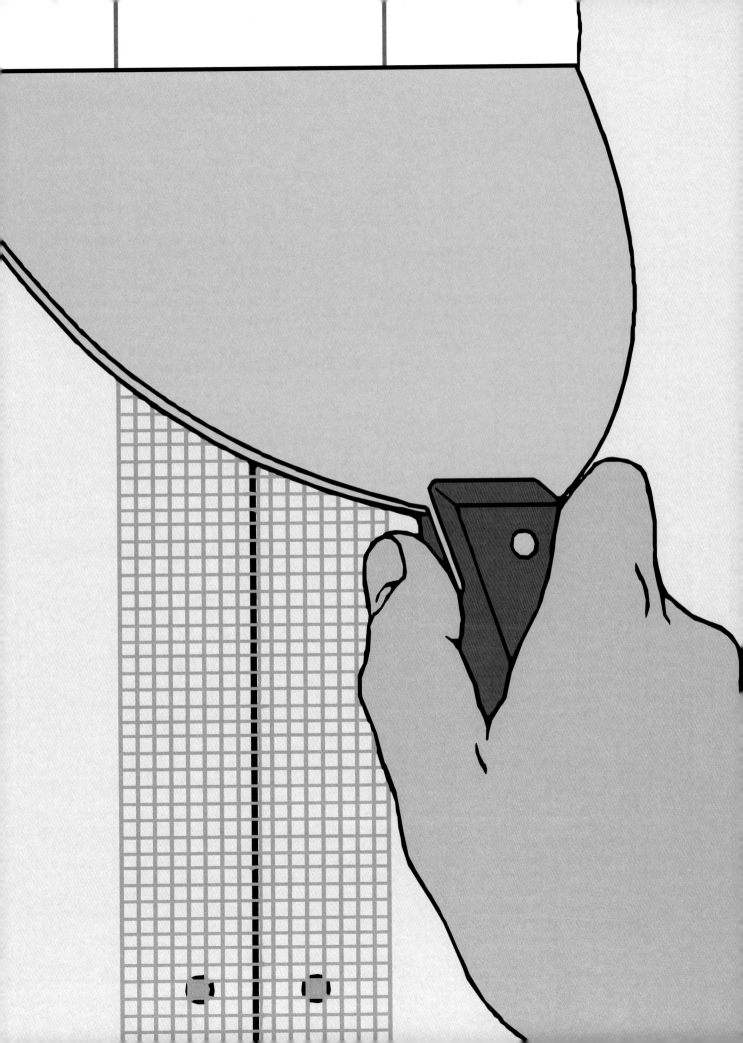

Building Partition Walls

The goal in dividing a room with a wall is to erect a sound structure that betrays nothing of its recent origins. In the construction methods shown on these pages, a wood frame is assembled flat on the floor from boards called studs fastened at the ends to boards known as the soleplate and the top plate. To install a doorway, follow the procedures on pages 34 and 35. When finished, the unit is tilted upright and attached to walls, ceiling, and floor.

Construction Variations: You can build a partition wall with metal studs and plates instead of wood *(page 29)*. With metal construction, you first attach the plates to the floor and ceiling and then you install the studs. This construction sequence is also use-ful when you are building with wood in a space that is too small for assembling the partition on the floor.

Adding Utilities: Metal studs are made with passages for wiring and plumbing, but you'll have to make openings in wood studs to accept utilities. It's best to consult a plumber if you plan to install pipes, but you can provide electricity to the new wall. Usually, power can come from an existing outlet box in a nearby circuit. Run the cable through holes drilled through the new wall studs to new outlet boxes installed on the studs of the open frame *(page 28)*. Postpone connecting the new circuit to the house supply until after you have covered the partition frame with wallboard and installed receptacles and switches.

 **TOOLS**

Combination square
Plumb bob
Circular saw
Framing hammer
Pry bar
Utility knife
Electric drill with $\frac{3}{4}$" bit

 **MATERIALS**

2 x 4s
Common nails ($3\frac{1}{2}$")
Cut nails ($2\frac{1}{2}$")
Cedar shims
Outlet boxes
Cable
Wire caps

 **SAFETY TIPS**

Protect your eyes with goggles and ears with earplugs when hammering and operating a circular saw. When using the saw add a dust mask to keep sawdust from your lungs.

⚠ CAUTION

Precautions for Lead and Asbestos

Lead and asbestos, known health hazards, pervade houses constructed or remodeled before 1978. Test all painted surfaces for lead with a test kit, available at hardware stores, or call your local health department or environmental protection office for other options. Potential asbestos locations include joint compound, ceiling and wall materials, insulation, and flooring and related adhesives. Mist such materials with a solution of 1 teaspoon low-sudsing detergent per quart of water to suppress dust, then remove small samples for testing by a National Institute of Standards and Technology-certified lab.

Hire a professional licensed in hazardous-substance removal for large jobs indoors, or if you suffer from cardiac, respiratory, or heat-tolerance problems that may be triggered by the protective clothing and respirator you must wear to do the work yourself. If you remove lead or asbestos yourself, follow these procedures:

❗ *Keep children, pregnant women, and pets out of the work area.*

❗ *Indoors, seal off openings to the work area from the rest of the house with 6-mil polyethylene sheeting and cut tape. Cover rugs and furniture that can't be removed with more sheeting and tape. Turn off air conditioning and forced-air heating systems.*

❗ *When you finish indoor work, mop the area twice, then run a vacuum cleaner equipped with a high efficiency particulate air (HEPA) filter.*

❗ *Outdoors, cover the ground in the work area with 6-mil polyethylene sheeting. Never work in windy conditions.*

❗ *If you must use a power sander on lead paint, get one equipped with a HEPA filter. Never sand asbestos-laden materials or cut them with power machinery. Mist them with water and detergent, and remove with a hand tool.*

❗ *Always wear protective clothing (available from a safety-equipment supply house or paint stores) and a dual-cartridge respirator. Remove the clothing—including shoes—before leaving the work area. Wash the clothing separately, and shower and wash your hair immediately.*

❗ *Dispose of the materials as recommended by your local health department or environmental protection office.*

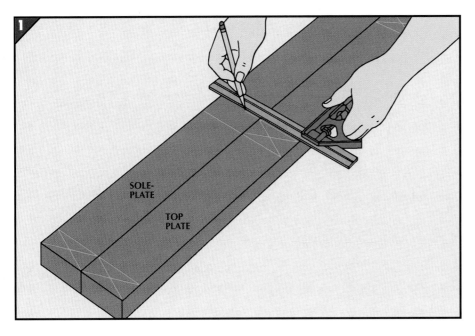

1. Marking the top plate and the sole plate.

◆ Measure the ceiling across which the new wall will run and cut two 2-by-4s to this length to serve as top plate and soleplate.

◆ Starting at one end of the top plate, mark stud locations $1\frac{1}{2}$ inches wide. Except at a doorway *(pages 34-35)*, space stud centers 16 inches apart, finishing with a stud location marked at the other end of the plate.

◆ With a combination square, transfer the markings from the top plate to the soleplate *(left)*.

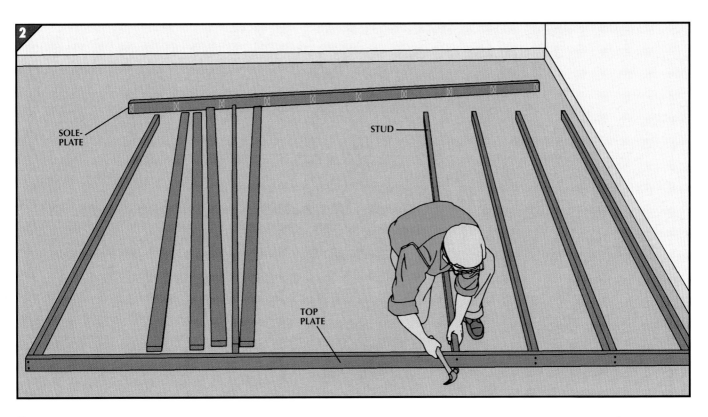

2. Assembling the frame.

◆ To determine the length of studs, measure along a plumb bob dropped from the ceiling to the floor at each end of the new wall and in the center.

◆ With a circular saw, cut 2-by-4 studs $3\frac{1}{4}$ inches shorter than the smallest of these measurements to allow for the combined thicknesses of the top plate and soleplate and for ceiling clearance when raising the wall.

◆ Turn any bowed studs so that they all curve in the same direction.

◆ Set the top plate on edge and fasten it to each stud with two $3\frac{1}{2}$-inch nails driven through the plate *(above)*. A framing hammer speeds the work.

◆ Nail the soleplate to the other ends of the studs in the same way.

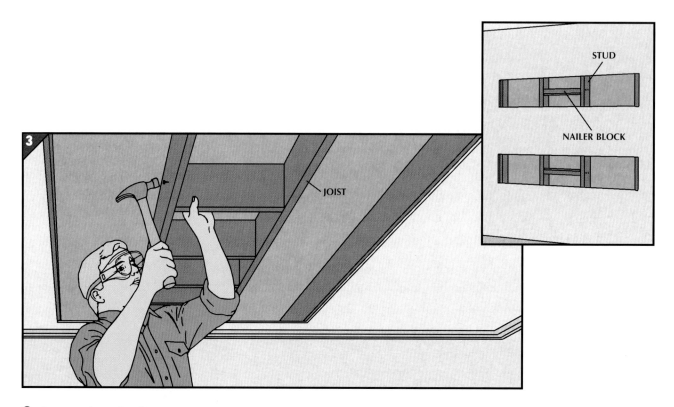

STUD

NAILER BLOCK

JOIST

3. Supporting the frame.

For a wall that will stand perpendicular to joists, mark the center of each joist on the ceiling *(page 8)*. Try to position a wall that parallels joists directly under one joist. If the wall runs between joists, install nailer blocks no more than 24 inches apart to support the frame *(above)*. Prepare truss or I-beam joists as shown on page 12.

◆ Cut the blocks from lumber the same size as the joists.

◆ If the space above the new wall is an unfloored attic, plan to install the blocks from above; if not, cut out a strip of ceiling 3 joist spaces wide as shown here.

◆ Set the bottoms of the blocks flush to the bottoms of the joists and fasten the blocks with two $3\frac{1}{2}$-inch nails in each end.

◆ After installing the blocks, patch the ceiling with wallboard *(pages 36-42)*, marking the patch with block locations before fastening it to the ceiling.

If the new wall meets an existing one between studs, cut slots in the wall for nailer blocks installed about one-third and two-thirds of the distance from floor to ceiling *(inset)*. Patch the slots with wallboard.

4. Removing baseboard.

For a tight fit between a new wall and an old one, remove the baseboard and shoe molding, a narrow strip often fastened at the bottom of the baseboard.

◆ Beginning at a corner or at a baseboard joint, gently loosen the baseboard and shoe molding where the new and old walls will intersect. Use a pry bar backed with a thin scrap of wood to avoid damaging the wall, and insert a wood wedge behind the baseboard to hold it away from the wall after you loosen it *(left)*.

◆ Repeat the process, inserting wedges as you go, until the strip is completely detached.

5. Securing the frame.

◆ With a helper, tilt the wall upright.
◆ While your helper holds the frame in place, push pairs of tapered cedar shims into each side of the gap between top plate and ceiling *(page 10)*. Place shims where you will nail the plate to joists or nailer blocks.
◆ Drive $3\frac{1}{2}$-inch nails through the top plate and shims, and into the joists or blocking overhead *(below)*; then score protruding shims with a utility knife and snap them off.
◆ Secure the soleplate to floor joists where possible; otherwise, nail it to the flooring. In either case, use $3\frac{1}{2}$-inch nails spaced 16 inches apart. For concrete floors, substitute $2\frac{1}{2}$-inch cut nails or use a powder-actuated hammer *(box, below)*.
◆ Fasten the end studs of the new wall to studs or nailer blocks in the existing one.

CEDAR SHIM

TOP PLATE

EXPLOSIVE POWER FOR NAILING TO CONCRETE

A powder-actuated hammer lets you drive a fastener through a soleplate and into a concrete floor with a single blow. Fit a special nail into the muzzle; a plastic spacer centers the nail in place. Then insert a power load—an explosive in a brass case—into the tool's chamber. To fasten a 2-by-4 soleplate to concrete, use $2\frac{1}{2}$-inch nails and No. 4 power loads. After closing the chamber, press the muzzle against the soleplate to release the tool's safety mechanism, and. strike a sharp blow with a 1-pound hammer. Doing so sets off the power load, which drives a piston that in turn drives the nail flush with the soleplate.

 CAUTION *Always wear ear protection and goggles when you use this tool.*

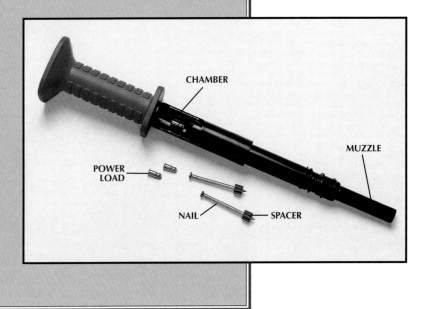

CHAMBER

MUZZLE

POWER LOAD

NAIL

SPACER

6. Turning a corner.

Add a stud and blocking to a corner *(right)* to reinforce the joint and provide nailing surfaces for wallboard.

◆ Cut two 2-by-4 nailer blocks about $3\frac{1}{2}$ inches long.

◆ Fasten the blocks to the end stud, one-third and two-thirds of the distance between floor and ceiling. Use $3\frac{1}{2}$-inch nails.

◆ Cut a stud and nail it to the nailer blocks. Then toenail it to the top plate and soleplate.

◆ Nail the end stud of the adjoining wall to the edges of nailing blocks and end stud at the reinforced corner.

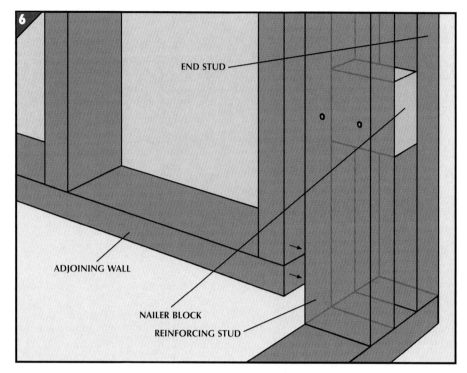

END STUD

ADJOINING WALL

NAILER BLOCK

REINFORCING STUD

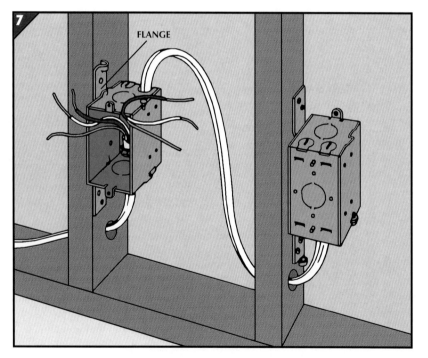

FLANGE

7. Roughing in wiring.

◆ Before covering the frame with wallboard, decide where you want switches and outlets in the new wall. Mark locations for them on the nearest studs.

◆ Determine where the new cable will tap into the house wiring, then drill $\frac{3}{4}$-inch holes through the studs of the new wall, near the soleplate, to accommodate the cable.

◆ Nail outlet boxes to the studs. Use boxes having flanges that position the front of the box flush with the wall surface after the wallboard is hung. Avoid placing outlet boxes that serve adjacent rooms within the same stud space; they will conduct sound from one room to the next.

◆ Run the cable, clamping it securely to each box *(left)*. Before hanging wallboard, tuck the wires out of the way inside the box.

After you install wallboard, switches, and receptacles, turn off the power to the circuit you intend to tap and use wire caps to connect the new cable—black wire to black, white to white, and ground to ground *(page 74)*.

FRAMING WITH METAL

Light-gauge metal studs and plates *(below)*, which are available from home centers, offer an attractive alternative to wood as a framing material for partition walls. Although unsuitable for supporting heavy bookshelves and cabinets, metal framing is less costly than wood and lighter in weight.

Like a partition framed in wood, a metal wall has a top plate at the ceiling and a soleplate fastened to the floor. Studs are attached to both plates at 24-inch intervals. All the pieces are cut to size with tin snips. Studs are tilted into position, then rotated perpendicular to the plates. End studs stand 2 inches from the wall; each end stud is put in place before the stud next to it, to make sure there is adequate working room.

All the studs are secured top and bottom with a $\frac{1}{2}$-inch No. 8 self-drilling pan-head sheet-metal screw in each side *(bottom photograph)*. Locking C-clamp pliers facilitate holding the stud in place while the screw is driven.

A doorway is framed by two metal studs and a metal header cut from the same stock as the plates, with a cripple stud between the header and the top plate; 2-by-4s screwed to the metal studs and header facilitate door installation *(top photograph)*.

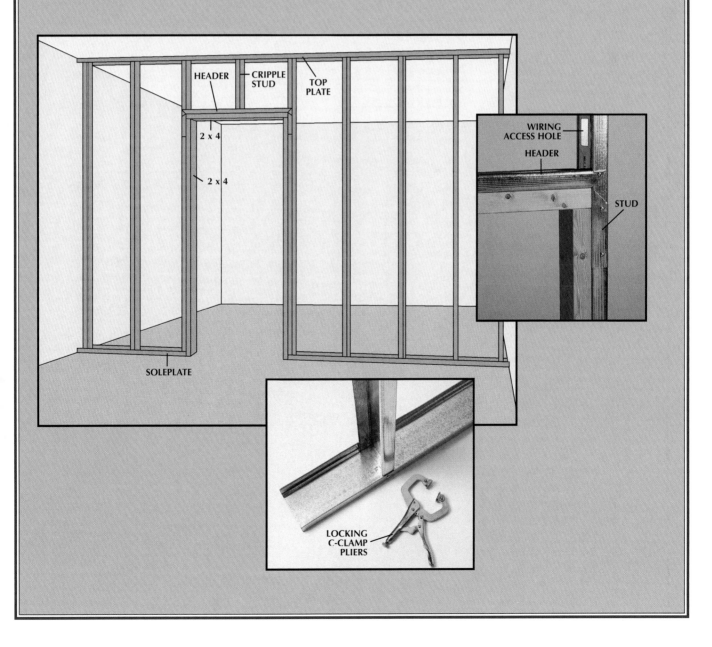

Framing for an Attic Room

The sloping roof of an attic poses problems in framing a new room, but they are easily solved by adapting the framing techniques shown on pages 24 to 29. At ceiling height, collar beams convert sloping surfaces to a horizontal one, with single-board beams functioning as joists for the ceiling and a doubled beam *(opposite, bottom)* providing a surface wide enough for attachment of the top plate of a center wall. At the room's sides, knee walls convert sloping surfaces to vertical ones.

Planning Considerations: A good ceiling height is $7\frac{1}{2}$ feet, but lower ceilings can work if the room has enough headroom, light, and ventilation. A knee wall 5 feet high is adequate for general use; low furniture such as a bunk bed or a storage chest may fit comfortably against even a 4-foot-high wall.

Working with Thick Rafters: In a home built before 1970, rafters may be thicker than present-day lumber. Thicken the blocking pieces between the boards of the doubled collar beam with scrap lumber. At the knee walls, center the studs when you toe-nail them into the rafters.

 **TOOLS**

Tape measure	Circular saw
Carpenter's level	Hammer
Chalk	Plumb line

 **MATERIALS**

Cardboard
Scrap lumber
Framing lumber (2 x 2, 2 x 4, 2 x 6)
Nails ($2\frac{1}{2}$", 3", $3\frac{1}{2}$")

SAFETY TIPS

Protect your eyes with goggles as you hammer, and put on a hard hat when you work with unsecured lumber overhead. A dust mask can make you more comfortable in an old attic.

PUTTING UP COLLAR BEAMS

1. Measuring and marking.
◆ Add the thickness of the planned ceiling material to the proposed ceiling height and cut a length of scrap lumber to that length.
◆ Stand the board upright against each rafter located in the planned area for the room. Use a level to make sure the board is vertical, and mark the rafter where it and the top of the board intersect *(right)*.

Using another piece of scrap lumber in the same way, mark the rafters for the tops of the knee walls.

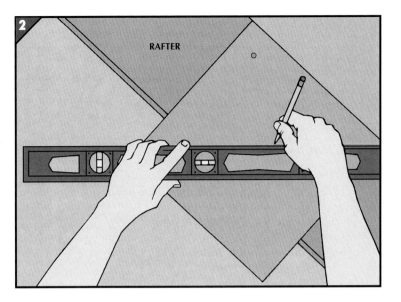

2. Making a pattern for the beam ends.

The collar beams must be beveled to provide the maximum nailing surface and to avoid splitting the beam ends. Create a pattern for the bevel as follows:

◆ Tack a square of cardboard to a rafter, placing one edge flush with the outside edge of the rafter.
◆ Hold a level against the square, with one corner of the level at the outermost corner of the square. From this corner draw a horizontal line (left).
◆ Detach the square, cut along the line, and discard the lower portion.
◆ On both sides of the remaining piece, mark with chalk along the newly cut edge and the edge that was tacked flush with the rafter edge.

If the pitch of the opposite roof is at a different angle, make an additional pattern.

3. Cutting the beam.

◆ At the pair of rafters above the planned center wall, locate the ceiling-height marks made in Step 1. Measure from the outside edge of one rafter to the outside edge of the opposite rafter at that height. Then subtract $\frac{1}{2}$ inch.
◆ Cut two 2-by-6 boards to that length.
◆ Place the apex of the angle formed by the two chalked edges of the pattern at one end of one of the boards.
◆ Hold either of the two chalked edges of the pattern flush with the bottom edge of the board.

◆ Draw a pencil line along the other chalked edge of the pattern (above).
◆ Mark the other end of the board

in a similar fashion.
◆ Cut the board at the diagonal lines.
◆ Cut the second board the same way.

4. Installing the beam.

◆ Fasten the cut boards to either side of the selected rafters with three 3-inch nails at the boards' ends; place each board so the bottom is at the ceiling-height marks and there is a space of $\frac{1}{4}$ inch between the beam ends and the roof (left).
◆ If the collar-beam span is 8 feet or more, nail short blocks of 2-by-4 between the boards at 3- to 4-foot intervals to keep them from bowing.

CONSTRUCTING THE WALLS

1. Building knee walls.
◆ On one of the center-wall rafters, locate the mark made for a knee wall *(page 30)*. Drop a plumb line to the joist below; mark the joist.
◆ Measure in from the outside end of that joist to the mark. To position the other end of the knee wall, measure in from the end of that joist by the same amount.
◆ From the outside face of the collar-beam rafter, measure off the length of the knee wall. Cut a 2-by-4 to that length for the soleplate.

◆ Fasten the plate to the floor with 3-inch nails at 1-foot intervals; add $3\frac{1}{2}$-inch nails over each joist.
◆ At each rafter, rest a vertical length of 2-by-4 on the soleplate, plumb it with a level, and trace the angle of the rafter on the 2-by-4 *(right)*.
◆ Cut the 2-by-4 on the diagonal line.
◆ Set the stud in place. Attach the top to the rafter with two 3-inch nails, then toenail the base to the soleplate.
◆ Build the other knee wall the same way.

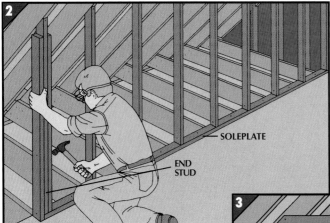

SOLEPLATE

END STUD

2. Completing the wall.
Make nailing surfaces for wallboard at the end of each knee wall as follows:
◆ At the back of the end stud, measure the distances from the rafter to the floor on one side, and from the rafter to the soleplate on the other.
◆ Cut a 2-by-4 to each length.
◆ Nail them to the sides of the end stud with $2\frac{1}{2}$-inch nails *(left)*.

3. Assembling the center wall.
◆ Measure the distance from the outside edge of one knee wall to the outside edge of the other; cut a 2-by-4 to this length to serve as the soleplate for the center wall. For a door, cut kerfs in the plate as shown on page 35.
◆ Measure the bottom of the doubled collar beam from rafter to rafter and cut a 2-by-4 to this length as a top plate.
◆ Measure from the bottom of the beam to the floor at several points. Take the shortest distance and subtract $3\frac{1}{4}$ inches. Then cut studs to that length.
◆ Build this part of the wall on the attic floor as you would a conventional partition *(pages 24-29)*. Frame for a door opening as shown on page 35.
◆ Raise the wall and position it so that

the soleplate meets the outside end of the thickened knee-wall stud.
◆ Shim the top plate as needed and

then nail it in place *(above)*.
◆ Nail the soleplate to the floor with 3-inch nails at 1-foot intervals.

4. Thickening the rafter.

◆ Measure along the rafter from the end of the doubled collar beam to the end stud of the knee wall; cut two 2-by-2s or 2-by-4s to that length to serve as nailers.

◆ Attach the nailers to opposite sides of the rafter with $2\frac{1}{2}$-inch nails, positioning the bottoms flush with the bottom of the rafter.

◆ Cut a 2-by-4 to run from the center wall to the knee wall as a top plate, angling one end to fit tightly against the knee-wall stud.

◆ Nail the top plate against the rafter and nailers.

◆ Thicken the rafter in the other part of the wall in the same way.

5. Completing the center wall.

◆ At each side of the center wall, mark the sole-plate for a stud next to the knee-wall corner and for any additional studs between that point and the existing full-length studs.

◆ Set lengths of 2-by-4 vertically on 2-by-4 scraps next to the marks, trace the height and angle of the rafter at the upper ends, and cut the 2-by-4s at the trace marks for studs.

◆ Toenail the studs into place between the top plate and soleplate with 3-inch nails; for a tight joint, fasten the first stud to the knee-wall corner with four $2\frac{1}{2}$-inch nails.

After the walls are complete, frame for the ceiling by installing a single collar beam at each rafter pair, following the nailing pattern shown in the inset.

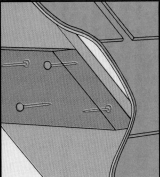

Making a Place for a Door

When your plans call for either an open passageway or a door between rooms, a supporting structure called a rough doorframe replaces one or more studs in the partition wall *(pages 24-27)*. Ideally, one of the regular wall studs can serve as a king stud for the doorframe. The location of cripple studs should maintain standard stud spacing along the wall.

A Place for a Prehung Door: If you buy a complete prehung unit, you can make precise framing calculations in advance, as explained below, even though the door will not be installed until wallboard is in place. At each step of construction, check the frame with a square to make sure the finished opening will be level and plumb.

An Open Passageway: If you plan a passageway finished with wallboard *(pages 36- 42)*, a simple formula applies: The distance between the king studs should be 4 inches wider than the intended width of the opening; this allows room for the jack studs and a $\frac{1}{2}$-inch layer of wallboard on each side.

 TOOLS

Circular saw   Carpenter's square
Framing hammer   Handsaw

 MATERIALS

Common nails ($2\frac{1}{2}$", $3\frac{1}{2}$")
2 x 4s

 **SAFETY TIPS**

When sawing lumber and hammering nails, wear goggles to protect your eyes.

A rough frame.

In a new partition wall, a doorway is framed between king studs and adjoining jack studs, both resting on the soleplate. The jack studs support a crosspiece called a header, which forms the top of the frame. Short studs called cripples brace the header against the top plate and provide nailing surfaces for wallboard above the door.

If a prehung door will be installed, the distance between the king studs should be $3\frac{1}{2}$ inches wider than the unit (shown at right with the casing removed for clarity). The jack studs are cut $1\frac{1}{4}$ inches shorter than the height of the

top jamb, allowing $1\frac{1}{2}$ inches for the thickness of the soleplate, less $\frac{1}{4}$ inch for clearance above the jamb. When completed, the rough frame is $\frac{1}{4}$ inch higher and $\frac{1}{2}$ inch wider than the door unit, allowing for shimming.

During construction of the frame, the continuous soleplate of the partition wall is partially cut: At the inside edge of each side of the planned frame opening, a kerf is sawed from the bottom surface of the soleplate to within $\frac{1}{4}$ inch of its upper surface *(Step 1, opposite, inset)*. After the partition wall is raised, these cuts are completed to free the waste section.

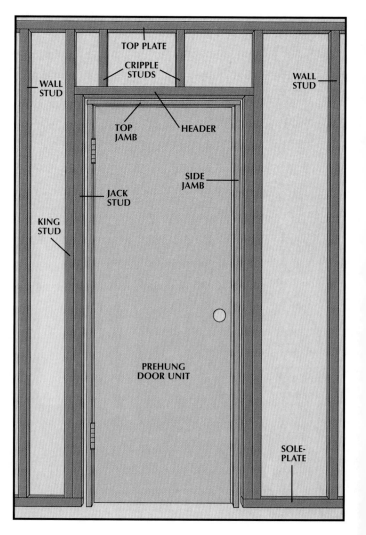

34

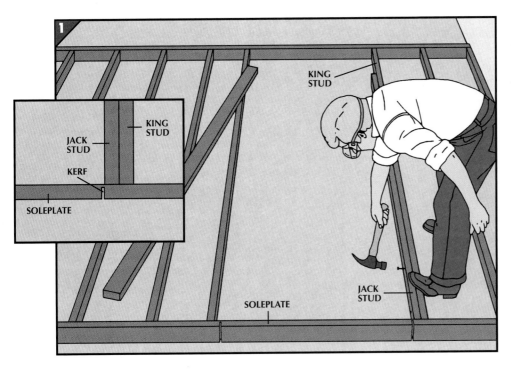

1. Installing the jack studs.

◆ Against a king stud in the partially built partition wall, lay a jack stud on the soleplate, with its bottom end aligned with the sawn kerf *(inset)*. Drive two $3\frac{1}{2}$-inch nails through the soleplate into the jack stud.
◆ Brace the king stud with your foot *(left)* and nail the jack stud to the king stud with six $2\frac{1}{2}$-inch nails at 1-foot intervals.
◆ Attach the other jack stud in the same way.

2. Installing the header.

◆ Cut a 2-by-4 to fit snugly between the two king studs.
◆ Lay the header across the tops of the jack studs and nail it in place with two $3\frac{1}{2}$-inch nails driven through each king stud.

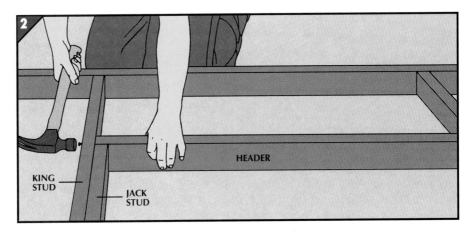

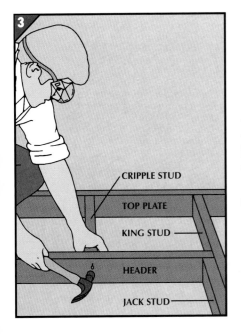

3. Installing the cripple studs.

◆ Cut cripple studs to fit between the header and the top plate.
◆ Position these studs at the 16- or 24-inch intervals of regular wall studs and secure them with $3\frac{1}{2}$-inch nails driven through the top plate and the header.
◆ After raising the wall into position *(page 27)*, use a handsaw to complete the kerf cuts and free the unwanted section of the soleplate at the base of the opening.

Hanging Wallboard

Wallboard—also called dry wall—is the common-sense solution for sheathing interior walls. Consisting of a core of gypsum sandwiched between layers of heavy paper, a standard sheet of wallboard is 4 feet wide, 8 feet long, and $\frac{1}{2}$ inch thick. It is also available in larger sheets—10 and 12 feet long and $4\frac{1}{2}$ feet wide—and in varying thicknesses. For most walls, $\frac{1}{2}$-inch-thick wallboard is suitable.

Preparing: Estimate your needs by calculating the square footage of each wall, ignoring all openings except the largest, such as picture windows. Convert this figure into sheets by dividing it by the square footage of a panel.

Before covering exterior walls, check to make sure that the wall is insulated *(pages 106-108)*.

Vertical versus Horizontal: In any dry-wall installation, vertical seams must align with the centers of studs. In most cases, this is easier to accomplish when the boards are laid horizontally *(page 39)*; however, for a narrow wall you can avoid creating a seam if you lay the sheet vertically *(page 38)*.

Concealing Fasteners and Joints: Nailheads or screwheads are hidden with a filler called joint compound, whereas seams between sheets are covered with paper or fiberglass joint tape before the compound is applied *(pages 41-42)*. Outside corners must be strengthened with angled metal strips called corner bead *(page 42)*.

 TOOLS

Tape measure
Framing square
Utility knife
Pocket plane
Caulking gun
Hammer or dry-wall hammer
Chalk line
Dry-wall saw
Wallboard saw
Taping knives (6", 10")
Joint compound pan
Wallboard sponge

 **MATERIALS**

Wallboard
Scrap 2 x 4s
Wallboard adhesive
Scrap shingle
Ring-shank wallboard nails or
   wallboard screws ($1\frac{1}{2}$")
Common nails ($2\frac{1}{2}$")
Electrical outlet box
Joint tape (fiberglass and
   precreased paper)
Joint compound
Corner bead

 **SAFETY TIPS**

Goggles are necessary when nailing and when working above eye level.

Six Tips for a Smooth Job

✔ Buy wallboard with the long edges tapered for ease in finishing the joints.

✔ Use self-adhesive joint tape on flat seams—it is easier to apply than plain tape; precreased paper tape works better for inside corners.

✔ Choose premixed joint compound rather than the dry form—it will retain its consistency and moisture if you reseal the container carefully.

✔ Stack and store wallboard flat on the floor indoors to prevent it from getting wet and from bowing or breaking.

✔ Cut wallboard short instead of long to fit into a given area, and leave a $\frac{1}{16}$-inch gap around sheets. Trying to force wallboard into too small a space crumbles the edges.

✔ Don't rush the job. Taking nailing shortcuts or ignoring wrinkled joint tape or uneven joint compound might save installation time but can result in split joints and popping nails.

CUTTING THE SHEETS

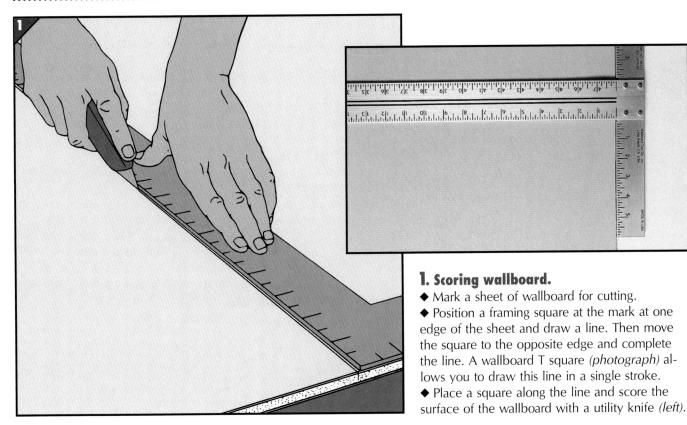

1. Scoring wallboard.
◆ Mark a sheet of wallboard for cutting.
◆ Position a framing square at the mark at one edge of the sheet and draw a line. Then move the square to the opposite edge and complete the line. A wallboard T square *(photograph)* allows you to draw this line in a single stroke.
◆ Place a square along the line and score the surface of the wallboard with a utility knife *(left)*.

2. Snapping the core.
◆ Stack two 2-by-4 scraps under the wallboard just behind the scored line.
◆ With the palm of your hand, hit the short end of the sheet, snapping the core.
◆ Finish by slicing through the backing with a utility knife, then trim any ragged paper from the cut edge.

LEVER —————— FULCRUM

1. Positioning the first sheet.

◆ Mark the ceiling and floor to indicate the centers of the studs and prepare any electrical outlet boxes for marking *(page 40)*.

◆ To test-fit the sheet, lean it into position at an inside corner. Raise the sheet to the ceiling with a foot lever made from a piece of wood shingle that pivots on a scrap-wood fulcrum.

◆ Trim the sheet as needed with a pocket plane *(photograph)* to ensure a $\frac{1}{2}$-inch gap between the floor and the bottom of the sheet.

◆ Apply a $\frac{3}{8}$-inch-thick zigzag bead of wallboard adhesive to each stud behind the sheet with a caulking gun. Start and stop the bead 6 inches short of the stud ends so the adhesive will not ooze out at the joints.

◆ Lift the panel to the ceiling, aligning the outer edge with the centerline of the stud as you do so. Press the sheet against the studs.

◆ Using the stud marks on the ceiling as a guide, nail or screw the wallboard to each stud about 1 foot below the ceiling.

2. Fastening the board.

◆ Secure the panel to each stud with ring-shank nails or wallboard screws spaced about 2 feet apart, starting 1 inch from the top and ending 1 inch from the bottom, and double the fasteners at the midsection of the sheet. Drive nails and screws straight; angled fasteners can break the paper covering *(top inset)*. If a nail or screw misses a stud, remove the fastener and try again; you can fill the hole later with joint compound.

◆ Drive nails flush, then dimple them—hammer the heads a fraction of an inch below the surface *(center inset)*. Do not strike so hard that you break the paper covering *(bottom inset)*. Tighten screws to countersink the heads just below the wallboard surface, without damaging the paper cover.

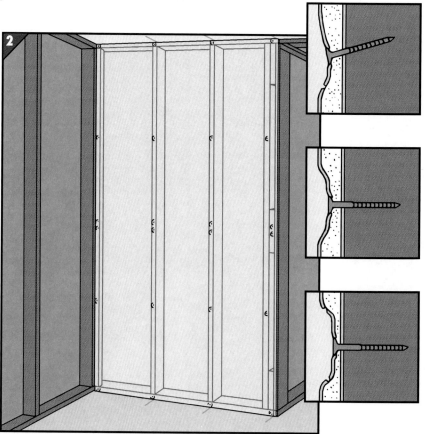

A Quick Way to Drive Screws

Dry-wall screws can be driven into wallboard speedily with an electric screw gun designed for this purpose. However, if you have a variable-speed drill, you can adapt it for wallboard screws with an attachment called a dimpler *(photograph)*. Like a screw gun, the dimpler has a depth stop and a clutch that disengages when a screw is driven to just below the wall surface.

DIMPLER

HANGING SHEETS HORIZONTALLY

Putting up the panels.

◆ Mark the stud positions on the ceiling and floor.

◆ Drive $2\frac{1}{2}$-inch common nails partway into the studs—4 feet below the ceiling for 4-foot-wide sheets ($4\frac{1}{2}$ feet for the wider panels).

◆ Unless you are positioning the board to mark an electrical outlet *(page 40)*, apply adhesive to the studs *(Step 1, opposite)*.

◆ With a helper, lift the wallboard to the ceiling, and rest it on the nails. Align the vertical edge with the center of a stud.

◆ Nail or screw the panel to each stud about a foot from the ceiling. After driving the rest of the fasteners *(Step 2, opposite)* remove the support nails.

◆ Because ceilings and floors are rarely parallel, measure from the bottom of the sheet to the floor in at least four places and mark these distances on the second sheet.

◆ If the distances are fairly uniform, snap a chalk line between the marks, then score and break the second sheet at the chalk line *(page 37)*. Otherwise, connect the marks with separate straight lines and cut the sheet with a dry-wall saw.

◆ If you will be putting up adjacent horizontal sheets, trim the second sheet to a length one stud shorter than the sheet above to stagger upper and lower joints. Also shave the panel lengthwise as needed to create a $\frac{1}{2}$-inch gap between the wallboard and the floor.

◆ With a helper, raise the sheet with a couple of foot levers *(Step 1, opposite)* and fasten it to the studs.

ELECTRICAL OUTLETS

1. Marking the position.

◆ Fold the wires into the outlet box.

◆ Remove the mounting screws from the outlet-box ears and insert them from back to front through their holes so that they protrude about $\frac{1}{2}$ inch *(right)*.

◆ Place the wallboard sheet in its proper position against the wall *(page 38 or 39)* and press it against the screw tips.

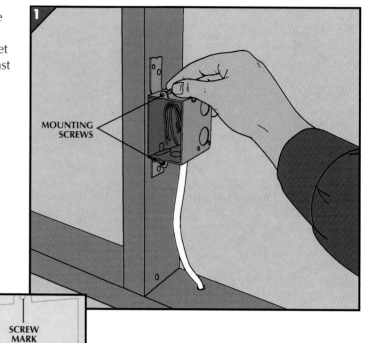

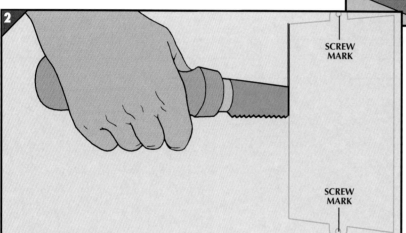

2. Cutting the hole.

◆ Remove the sheet and place a spare outlet box on the wallboard, aligning the mounting holes with the marks made by the screws, then trace around the box.

◆ Force a wallboard saw through the board and cut just outside the lines, angling the saw so that the hole is slightly wider at the back of the sheet.

◆ Trim off any ragged paper around the cut and install the sheet *(pages 38-39)*.

DOORS AND WINDOWS

Marking and cutting the opening.

For a window, measure from the ceiling to the top of the jamb at both corners. Next, measure from the last installed sheet to the nearest side-jamb edge. If the sheet will surround the window, also measure to the farthest side-jamb edge. For a door, measure the distances from the ceiling to the top jamb and from the last installed sheet to the side-jamb edge or edges.

◆ Mark these distances on the face of the sheet and connect the marks.

◆ If the sheet will enclose three sides of the window or door, cut along the two parallel lines with a dry-wall saw.

◆ Score the remaining line and snap the core *(page 37, Steps 1 and 2)*. If the sheet will surround a window, cut around all the lines with the saw.

◆ Similarly, mark and cut the lower sheet *(right)*.

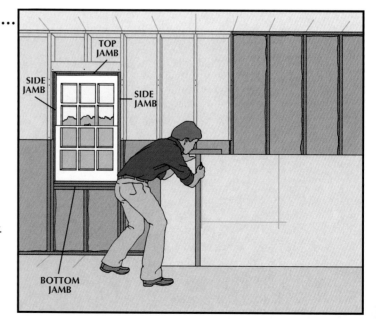

CONCEALING JOINTS AND FASTENERS

1. Taping the joint.
◆ Press the end of a roll of self-adhesive fiberglass-mesh joint tape against the top of the joint.
◆ Unwind the tape with one hand and use a taping knife to press the tape to the joint. Watch for wrinkles; if they appear, lift the tape, pull it tight, and press it again.
◆ Cut the tape off the roll when you reach the end of the joint.

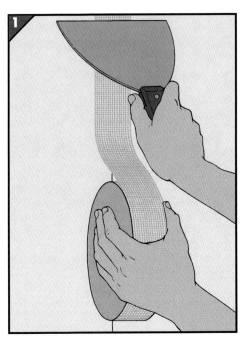

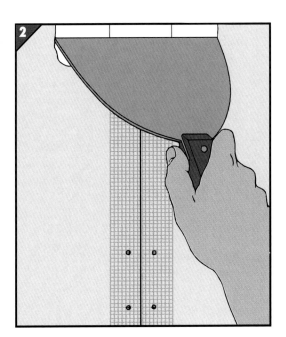

2. Applying joint compound.
◆ Use the same knife to spread compound over the joint tape and the adjacent wallboard in a layer approximately $\frac{1}{16}$ inch thick. On joints where nontapered ends of dry wall abut, apply compound slightly thicker. While working, wipe the knife frequently against the lip of the pan; otherwise the compound will harden on the knife and score grooves in the wet compound.
◆ When the tape is covered, run the knife down the joint in one motion to smooth out the surface.

3. Feathering the joint.
Run a clean 10-inch knife down each side of the joint, spreading the compound outward. Press hardest on the outer side of the knife so the mixture gradually spreads to a feathered edge. Let the compound dry for a day.

Meanwhile, hide fastener heads elsewhere by drawing joint compound across each one with a 6-inch knife held nearly parallel to the wallboard. Then raise the knife blade to a steeper angle and scrape off excess compound with a stroke at right angles to the first.

Apply a second coat of joint compound thinned with about a pint of water per 5 gallons. Using a 10-inch taping knife, feather the compound to a distance of about 10 inches on either side of the joint. Where nontapered ends of dry wall abut, apply more compound and feather it to about 20 inches on each side of the joint.

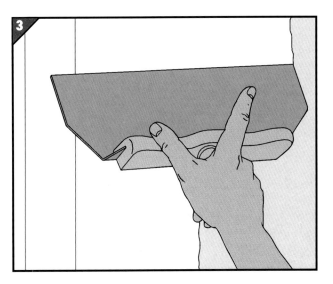

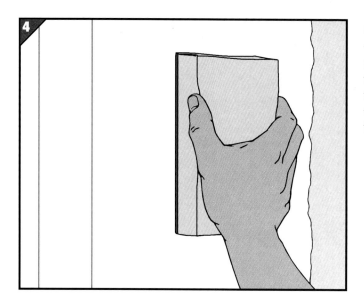

4. Smoothing the surface.

◆ When the last coat of joint compound is completely dry, rub it gently with a damp wallboard sponge. Be careful not to get the wallboard paper wet enough to tear, and rinse the sponge frequently.

◆ Repeat the procedure on the compound you applied to fastener heads.

DEALING WITH CORNERS

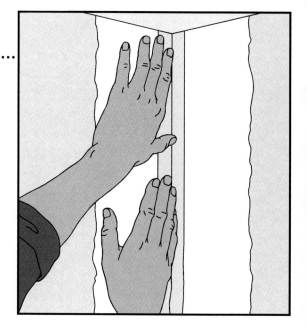

Taping inside corners.

◆ With a 6-inch taping knife, slather joint compound crosswise into the crack at an inside corner between two walls or a wall and the ceiling.

◆ After applying the compound, run the knife along each side of the joint to smooth the surface.

◆ Bend a length of paper tape in half down its crease line, and press the fold lightly into the corner by running your fingers along the joint.

◆ Draw the knife along each side of the corner, simultaneously embedding the tape and coating it lightly with compound.

◆ When applying the second and third coats use thinned compound *(page 41, Step 3)*. Do one side of the corner, allow the compound to dry 1 day, then do the other side.

◆ Smooth the compound with a wallboard sponge after it has dried *(Step 4, above)*.

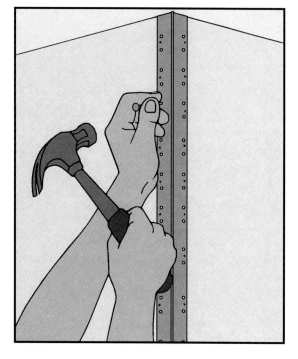

Strengthening outside corners.

◆ Nail a strip of metal corner bead so it fits flat on both sides of the corner.

◆ Load the left two-thirds of a 6-inch taping knife with joint compound.

◆ With the right half of the blade overhanging the corner, run the knife from ceiling to floor down the left side of the bead, smoothing the compound over the perforations.

◆ Cover the right side of the bead similarly.

◆ Clean the blade, then smooth and feather the joint by running the knife down each side of the bead.

◆ Let the compound dry for 1 day, then apply a second coat of thinned compound *(page 41, Step 3)*, feathering the edge about $1\frac{1}{2}$ inches beyond the dry compound.

◆ Wait 1 day, then apply a third coat using a 10-inch knife to feather the compound 2 inches farther on each side.

◆ Smooth the compound after it has dried *(Step 4, above)*. If the rounded tip of the metal bead still shows, it can be painted later with the rest of the wall.

A Factory-Fitted Door

Prehung doors eliminate most of the work that was once required to install and fit a new door. Clearances are machine checked and casings are already attached to the jamb, which comes in two interlocking halves. To erect the door, you simply pull the two halves apart, push one half into each side of the door opening, make adjustments, and nail the assembly in place.

Purchase Options: Most home centers stock prehung doors in at least two styles: louvered and flush. Doors are 6 feet 8 inches high and come in a variety of widths: 24 inches for closets and small bathrooms, 32 inches for most other rooms, and 30 inches for locations where a wider door would obstruct traffic when open. For walls covered with wallboard, buy a door with a $4\frac{5}{8}$-inch jamb. Plaster walls are thicker and commonly require a $5\frac{3}{8}$-inch jamb. Both right-handed and left-handed doors are available; to make sure you order the correct one, consult the box below.

When to Install: Put in the door after the wallboard or other wall covering is complete but before you install new flooring or baseboard. Once the carpet or other floor covering is in place, you may need to trim the bottom of the door for clearance *(page 45)*.

Prehung doors often come with holes predrilled in order to accommodate a standard lockset. After installing the door, put in a lockset according to the manufacturer's instructions.

 TOOLS

Hammer
Utility knife
Nail set
Screwdriver
Framing square
Circular saw with a fine-toothed blade

 **MATERIALS**

Wood shims
Finishing nails ($2\frac{1}{2}$", $3\frac{1}{2}$")
Wood putty

 **SAFETY TIPS**

Protect your eyes with safety goggles as you hammer nails or saw lumber.

WHICH WAY WILL IT OPEN?

Before buying a door, stand in the rough opening with your back against the intended hinge location. Extend an arm in the direction you would like the door to swing. If you reach to the right, as pictured here, the door is considered right-handed; if you reach to the left, it is left-handed.

As you stand in the opening, double-check whether the door will create an obstruction. Two open doors may block each other, a bathroom door may bump into the sink, and any door may hide a light switch or thermostat. Selecting a door that opens the other way—or installing the hinges on the opposite side—may solve the problem.

A prehung door.

This prefabricated unit consists of a door hinged at the factory to the inside of a jamb, with the casing and doorstop attached. The jamb comes split so that the halves can be pushed into the rough door opening from opposite sides. The doorstop hides the tongue-and-groove joint that joins the two halves. Before installing such a door, separate the jamb halves by removing the shipping braces and pulling the nail that holds the door closed.

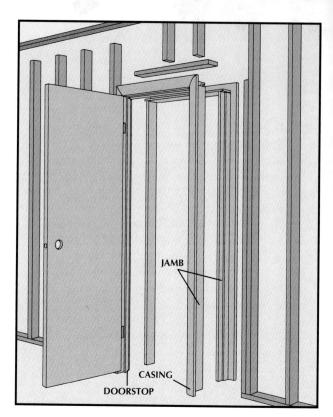

INSTALLING THE JAMB

1. Setting the door in place.

◆ Slide the half jamb attached to the door into the rough-framed wall opening.
◆ Support the door on wood shims.
◆ If the door comes without cardboard strips inserted between the door and jamb, slip wood shims between the two to maintain a $\frac{1}{8}$-inch clearance (left).
◆ Avoid gaps greater than $\frac{1}{8}$ inch between the door and the top and strike sides of the jamb by adjusting the position of the jamb—it has about $\frac{1}{4}$ inch of play. If necessary, you can trim the bottom of one of the jamb legs to maintain even clearance at the top of the doorway after the side jambs are adjusted.
◆ Fasten the casing with $2\frac{1}{2}$-inch finishing nails driven every 12 inches into the 2-by-4 frame of the rough opening.

2. Shimming the jamb.

◆ On the other side of the opening, insert two shims between the top of the jamb and the rough-opening frame to prevent the jamb from bowing outward over the years. In a properly made rough frame for a door there is a space of $\frac{1}{4}$ to $\frac{1}{2}$ inch between the frame and the jamb (pages 34-35).
◆ Insert three more shims along each side of the jamb; on the hinge side, place two shims just below the hinges and the third in the center (left).
◆ Score the shims with a utility knife at the jamb's edge, then break off the protruding ends by smacking them with a hammer.
◆ At each shim, drive two $3\frac{1}{2}$-inch finishing nails through the jamb and shims and into the rough frame.

44

3. Completing the jamb.

◆ Slide the other half of the doorjamb into position, taking care to engage its tongue in the groove of the jamb half already in place *(right)*.

◆ Press the casing snugly against the wall and nail it in place with $2\frac{1}{2}$-inch finishing nails driven through the casing and into the framing every 12 inches.

◆ Drive $3\frac{1}{2}$-inch finishing nails through the jamb and into the rough framing at similar intervals.

◆ Remove the shims wedging the door closed.

◆ Set all nails with a nail set and cover the heads with wood putty.

FINE-TUNING THE FIT

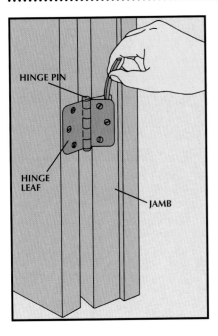

Making final adjustments.

Check the swing of the door to see whether it binds or is too far from the strike side of the jamb. Correct either problem as follows:

◆ Loosen the screws that anchor the hinge leaf to the jamb.

◆ Insert a narrow strip of cardboard behind the hinge leaf *(left)*. Position this shim along the edge near the hinge pin to move the door away from the hinge side of the jamb and toward the strike side; position it along the edge farthest from the pin to move the door in the opposite direction.

◆ Retighten the hinge-leaf screws.

The elimination of a bind at one point may create a bind at another. If you cannot straighten the door by shimming, remove it and plane the edges.

Trimming the bottom edge.

After flooring is installed, make sure the door is at least $\frac{1}{4}$ inch above the finish floor. If it is not, adjust the length of the door as follows:

◆ With the door in place, measure from the lower edge of the bottom hinge to the floor. Subtract $\frac{1}{4}$ inch.

◆ Insert a screwdriver below the cap of each hinge pin and tap it with a hammer. Lift the pins out and remove the door.

◆ Transfer the measurement onto the door's edge, measuring from the base of the hinge down. Extend the mark across the door with a framing square.

◆ Score the line with a utility knife to prevent chipping *(right)*.

◆ Cut along the line with a circular saw equipped with a fine-toothed blade.

◆ Slip the door back into place. Reseat the hinge pins.

Moldings for a Neat Finish

A room is not complete without baseboard molding installed along the bottoms of walls to cover the gap between the flooring and the wallboard. Base shoe at the baseboard and crown molding or cove molding around the ceiling add a touch of elegance.

The Order of Work: Nail baseboard and ceiling moldings in place after completing work on the walls, ceiling, and floor but before painting the room. Base shoe, which hides the joint between the baseboard and the floor, is generally stained and is installed after the room is painted.

At the Lumberyard: Baseboard and ceiling moldings are usually stocked in pine but can be ordered in other woods. Base shoe is readily available in oak to match wood floors.

Moldings come in precut lengths of 6, 8, 10, 12, 14, and 16 feet. For a neat job, plan your purchase to minimize splicing. Be sure to add 2 inches to room dimensions for each corner joint and each lap-joint splice *(opposite, bottom)* that you anticipate. And take into account that a splice in baseboards must fall at a stud. Since paint will hide lap joints but stain will not, avoid splicing base shoe if possible.

Essential Tools: The extra 2 inches at each joint are required for the angled cuts, or miters, required at splices and corners. To cut baseboard and crown molding miters, you need a backsaw and a miter box with a height-adjustable saw guide as shown on these pages. A coping saw is essential to complete a coped joint *(page 48)*, used at inside corners.

Fastening: Before nailing, remove any irregularities—such as accretions of paint on old walls or lumps of joint compound at the top or bottom of newly installed wallboard—that might prevent a tight fit. Nail with the same care used in cutting: A misplaced hammer blow can easily dent the soft pine of most molding.

 TOOLS

Miter box
Backsaw
Coping saw
Utility knife
Hammer
Nail set
Electric drill with $\frac{1}{16}$" bit

 MATERIALS

Baseboard
Base shoe
Ceiling molding
Finishing nails ($1\frac{1}{2}$", 2", $2\frac{1}{2}$", $3\frac{1}{4}$")
Wood filler

 **SAFETY TIPS**

Protect your eyes with safety goggles when drilling or hammering overhead.

MITERING FOR OUTSIDE CORNERS AND SPLICES

Cutting baseboard and base shoe.

◆ Place a length of molding against the wall and mark the top at the corner. For an additional length of molding, simply mark the correct length as described on the bottom of the opposite page.

◆ Set the saw guide at a 45-degree angle so that the front of the workpiece will be cut longer than the back. The dotted line in the inset shows the cut for the right-hand side of a corner.

◆ Raise the saw guide of the miter box high enough for the molding to stand upright. Place the molding in the box face outward, align the sawteeth with the cut mark, and make the cut.

◆ Adjust the miters to fit the corners as needed *(page 48)*.

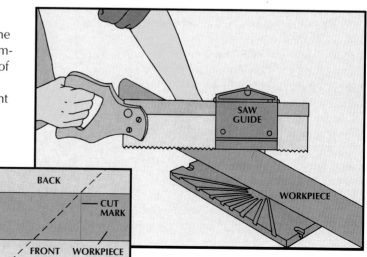

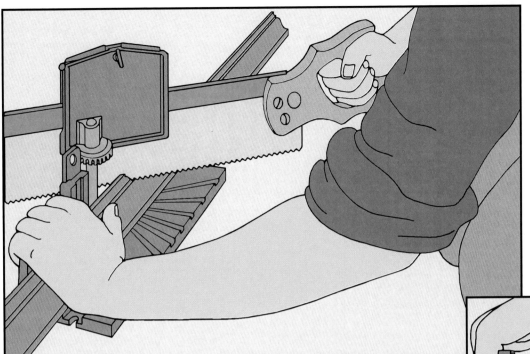

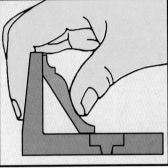

Cutting ceiling molding.

Crown and cove molding have flat surfaces at the top and bottom that rest against the ceiling and wall. For cutting, both are placed upside down in the miter box.

◆ Hold a length of crown molding against the ceiling and mark the molding's bottom edge at the corner of the wall; mark additional pieces to the correct length as described below.

◆ Place the molding upside down and face outward in the miter box, as if the bottom of the box were the ceiling (inset).

◆ Cut the molding so the front is longer than the back. Since the molding is upside down in the box, the saw shown above is angled correctly for the right-hand side of the corner.

◆ Adjust the miters to fit the corners as needed (page 48).

Splicing molding.

◆ For baseboard molding, locate a stud for nailing the splice.

◆ After mitering one end of a piece of molding for the preceding joint, place it against the wall and mark it across the top, at the stud center.

◆ Miter the molding at a 45-degree angle so that the cut bisects the mark.

◆ Miter another length of molding in the opposite direction, then mark and miter it for the next joint.

◆ Nail the first piece to the wall (page 49), then fit the second piece so that the angled cuts for the lap joint butt together. Drive a $1\frac{1}{2}$-inch finishing nail through the splice and into the center of the stud as shown here.

A splice in ceiling molding need not occur at a stud. When mitering ceiling molding for a lap joint, place it upside down in the miter box, as described at the top of this page.

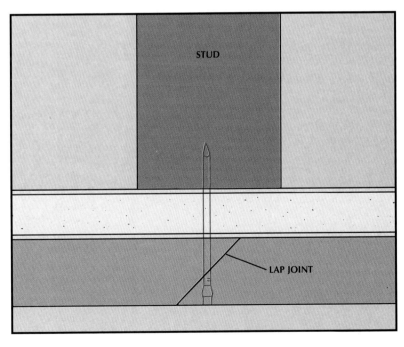

STUD

LAP JOINT

COPING AN INSIDE CORNER JOINT

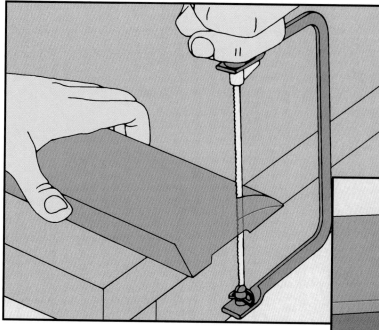

Cutting the pieces.

◆ Hold a piece of molding against one wall of the corner and butt the factory end against the adjacent wall. Cut the other end for the next joint, then nail the piece to the wall *(opposite, top)*.

◆ Miter the end of the other piece at a 45-degree angle, cutting it so that the back side of the molding will be longer than the front. Highlight the front edge of the cut with a pencil.

◆ Cut along the curve with a coping saw *(left)*, angled a few degrees to make the front of the molding piece longer than the back.

◆ Fit the shaped end against the molding already installed *(inset)*, then mark and cut the other end for the next joint.

◆ Nail the finished piece to each stud. Do not nail a coped joint at the corner.

MAKING OUTER CORNERS FIT EXACTLY

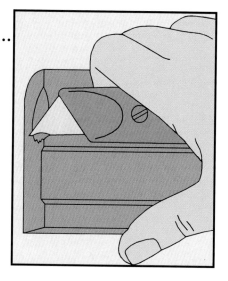

Feathering exterior angles.

To ease the fit of molding at outside corners, cut a crescent-shaped piece out of the mitered end of the molding with a utility knife or coping saw. Begin the cut half an inch below the top of the molding; cutting out any portion of the top will create a visible gap in the joint. Cut inward and down to the bottom.

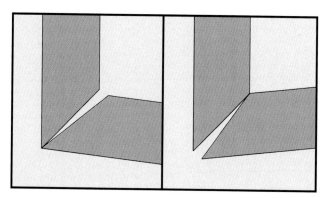

Matching angles to corners.

Since corners in a room seldom make exact 90-degree angles, mitered molding joints must usually be widened or narrowed to fit corners perfectly.

◆ If the joint gaps on the wall side *(far left)*, shave away the fronts of the angled cuts with a coping saw or utility knife.

Check the fit frequently while you work.

◆ When the joint gaps on the face side *(near left)*, shave away the back of the cuts in the same manner.

◆ Double-check the angles at both ends of each length of molding for fit before nailing the molding in place.

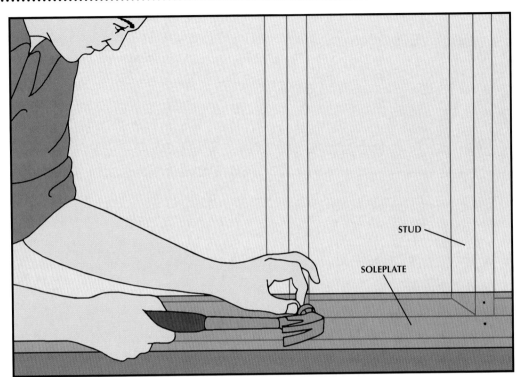

Fastening baseboard.
◆ Secure baseboard to the wall by driving two $2\frac{1}{2}$-inch finishing nails into the molding at each stud.
◆ Drive one of the nails through the middle of the molding, straight into the stud, and the other nail, at a 45-degree angle, into the soleplate near the bottom of the molding.
◆ Set the nails about $\frac{1}{8}$ inch into the wood with a nail set and fill the holes with wood filler.

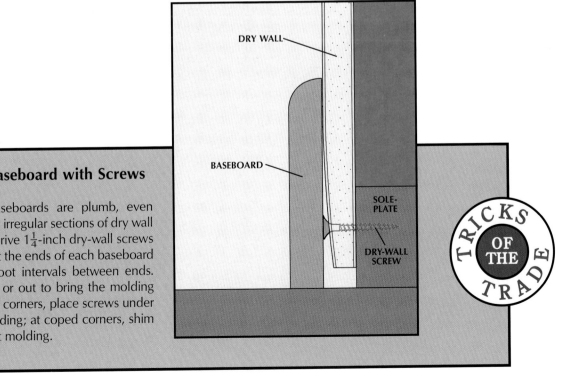

Fine-Tuning Baseboard with Screws

To ensure that baseboards are plumb, even when installed over irregular sections of dry wall or tapered edges, drive $1\frac{1}{4}$-inch dry-wall screws into the soleplate at the ends of each baseboard section and at 2-foot intervals between ends. Turn the screws in or out to bring the molding vertical. At mitered corners, place screws under both pieces of molding; at coped corners, shim only the square-cut molding.

TRICKS OF THE TRADE

CROWN MOLDING

Installing crown molding.

Nailing up long strips of molding works best when you have a helper to support one end. Begin work at a corner and work across the room to the opposite end.

◆ Hammer $3\frac{1}{4}$-inch finishing nails through the convex section near the center of the molding and into the top plate at approximately 16-inch intervals. To ensure hitting the plate, hold the nails at about a 45-degree angle.

◆ Countersink the nailheads with a nail set.

Creating a Shortcut for Nailing

For easier and faster installation of ceiling moldings, first attach a triangular wood nailer called a chamfer strip along the joint between wall and ceiling. Instead of passing through wallboard into the top plate, the nails securing the molding can then be sunk into the more accessible chamfer strip. Chamfer-strip nailers are especially useful on brittle plaster walls, where nailing could create unsightly cracks. Buy 1-inch chamfer strips from a lumberyard and secure them to the top plate with 2-inch dry-wall screws in plaster or 2-inch finishing nails in wallboard. Space fasteners at 2-foot intervals.

TRICKS OF THE TRADE

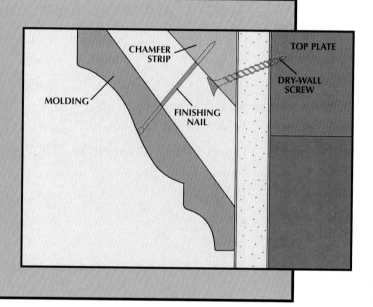

CHAMFER STRIP

MOLDING

FINISHING NAIL

TOP PLATE

DRY-WALL SCREW

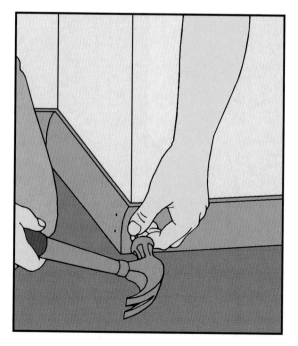

Finishing outside corners.

To secure mitered ends of baseboard and ceiling moldings, hammer two $1\frac{1}{2}$-inch finishing nails through the molding on each side of the corner, driving them into the corner stud inside the wall. Blunt all nail points with a hammer to prevent splitting the molding, and countersink the nailheads with a nail set.

Fastening base shoe.

Nail the base shoe to the floor with 1½-inch finishing nails spaced at intervals of about 16 inches.

◆ For pine base shoe, place the nail point just above the middle of the base shoe *(inset);* starting the nail too near the top of the shoe can split the wood. Drive each nail into the floor at about a 60-degree angle.

◆ For hardwood moldings, drill a pilot hole for each nail with a $\frac{1}{16}$-inch bit. Alternatively, use a nail spinner *(photograph),* a drill attachment that drives finishing nails through hardwoods without predrilling.

◆ Countersink the nailheads with a nail set.

NAIL SPINNER

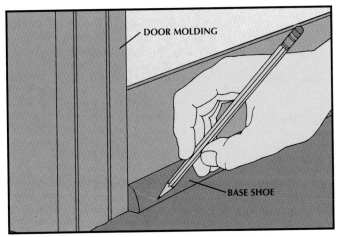

DOOR MOLDING

BASE SHOE

Shaping base shoe at doorways.

◆ To improve the appearance of base shoe that ends at a door molding *(left)* or built-in, sculpt the square-cut end of the base shoe into a graceful curve.

◆ Holding the base shoe in place, mark a freehand pencil line on the base shoe. Begin the line where the top of the base shoe meets the door molding, and curve the line away from the doorway.

◆ Set the base shoe on a solid surface, cut along the line with a coping saw, and sand the cut smooth.

MARRYING NEW TRIM TO OLD

When you add a partition to a room, you may be able to buy new moldings that match the old. If so, trim the old molding to butt against the inside corner formed with the new wall. Then join the new molding to the old with a coped joint.

In the case of an antique molding that you cannot match, substitute a plain new molding or clear pine board cut to the same height as the old molding. You can then butt the ends of the new molding against the existing walls and fit the antique moldings against the new with butt joints *(right).*

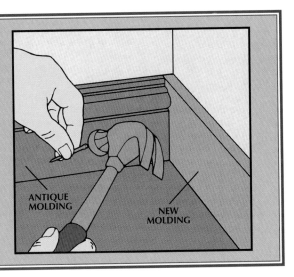

ANTIQUE MOLDING

NEW MOLDING

Removing Old Walls

Taking out a wall can turn two cramped rooms into an inviting, more useful one. Identify any complications before you start by inspecting the wall.

Dealing with Utilities: First, determine what may be inside the wall. The number of outlets and switches suggests how much wiring it contains. A bathroom above may be hooked to plumbing that descends through the wall. From the basement you may be able to detect whether heating pipes or ducts rise within the wall.

If all you find is wiring that terminates at outlets in the wall, you can remove the wires when you take out the wall *(opposite, bottom)*. A heat duct connected to a wall register can be cut back to the floor and capped with a register there. Even if a wall contains many pipes and cables, you may be able to remove most of the partition and leave one end to carry the lines, which can be moved by a plumber or an electrician.

Bearing or Nonbearing Walls: You must also determine a crucial fact—whether the wall bears weight from above, thus serving as a vital structural element of the house. The key clue to a bearing wall is joists crossing its top plates, perpendicular to them *(diagram, below)*. A nonbearing wall usually runs parallel to the joists and perpen-dicular to the long walls of the house.

You can detect joists by looking in the attic and basement or by cutting a small hole in the ceiling. If you find a girder or wall running under and parallel to the partition, you can also be sure it is a bearing wall. If any doubt remains, assume that the wall bears weight.

As shown at right and on pages 54 and 55, nonbearing walls can be removed in whole or in part as you prefer. To take out a bearing wall, consult pages 56 to 59. Such a wall must be replaced by framing near the ceiling that will be visible in the finished room.

Finishing the Job: After removing the wall, you will confront breaks in the ceiling, walls, and floor. Wallboard ceilings and walls are easy to patch *(pages 36-42)*. The break in the floor can be built up with any wood as thick as the flooring, and the whole room carpeted or tiled. Professional help may be needed for hardwood floors that will remain exposed.

 **CAUTION** Before starting work, check for lead and asbestos in the wall as explained on page 24.

 **CAUTION** Make sure power is off to all wiring in the wall before beginning work; turn off the power at the service panel, then check with a circuit tester at the wall.

 TOOLS

Circular saw
with metal-
cutting
blade
Circuit tester

Pry bar
Screwdriver
Handsaw
Crowbar
Hammer
Wallboard
knife

 **MATERIALS**

Drop cloths
and tape
Scrap lumber
Framing lumber
(2 x 4s, 2 x 8s,
2 x 10s)

Nails (2½")
Wallboard
Joint com-
pound
Joint tape
Corner bead

SAFETY TIPS

Demolition creates dust, flying splinters, and other potentially dangerous debris. Put on safety goggles, a dust mask, and leather work gloves. Long sleeves, long pants, and sturdy shoes are also in order, and a cap or scarf will keep the mess out of your hair.

Bearing and nonbearing walls.

In a typical frame house, represented at right in a simplified diagram, the roof is supported by long outer, or side, walls parallel to the ridge. The weight of the remaining structure—as well as the house contents—rests on joists, which transfer the load to the side walls. These walls pass the weight to the foundations and on to the footings. (End walls usually do not carry weight.) Since a standard wood joist cannot span the usual distance from one side wall to another, house framers provide two joists and rest their inside ends on an interior bearing wall. The interior bearing wall carries the weight down to a solid support, either to a bearing wall that rests on its own footings or, as shown here, to a girder with ends that rest on the foundation.

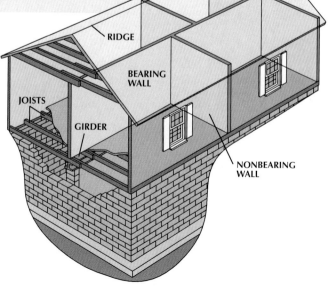

GETTING RID OF A NONBEARING WALL

1. Stripping the wall.

◆ Check for utility lines in the wall as described in the text at left, and deal with them as explained there. Make sure the power is off to outlets in the wall.

◆ Tear off the wall trim with a pry bar.
◆ Tape down drop cloths in each room, close any interior doors, and open the windows.
◆ Cut strips of wall from between the studs with a circular saw set to the thickness of the wall surface; use a metal-cutting blade if the wall is made of plaster on metal lath.
◆ Saw the studs in two near the middle, and work the halves free from their nailing *(above)*.

2. Removing outlet wiring.

◆ When you reach an outlet, remove its cover plate and strip off the wall surface around it.
◆ If the box is connected to a single cable coming up from a basement directly beneath, disconnect the cable from its receptacle and box. Then tug at it while a helper in the basement watches to identify it by its movement *(right)*.
◆ Trace the cable to the nearest electrical box, disconnect it, and pull it out of the wall.

You may need professional help to reroute the wiring if you cannot discover a cable's origin, if the outlet box has more than one cable entering it, or if unrelated cables pass through the wall.

TOP PLATE

3. The last stud.

◆ Work the bottom of the end stud loose from the wall with a pry bar, using a wide wood scrap against the adjoining wall as a fulcrum to protect the surface.
◆ Continue to pry up the stud by making use of a pry bar and wood scrap.

◆ When the stud is safely away from the wall, wrench it free *(left)*.

The top plate is often nailed upward to blocks between adjacent joists. Pry it down, beginning at the nailhead nearest one end, using a wood scrap as a prying surface to protect the ceiling.

4. The soleplate.

◆ Somewhere near the center of the soleplate, make two saw cuts about 2 inches apart.
◆ Chisel out the wood between the cuts down to the subfloor.
◆ Insert a crowbar and pry up one end of the plate *(above)*. With a scrap of 2-by-4 as a fulcrum, pry up the other end.

Repair the gaps made in the adjoining walls and the ceiling as described in the text on page 52. If you are planning to cover the floor with resilient tiles, wood parquet, or carpeting, fill in the space where the soleplate rested with a board thick enough to make the surface even.

LEAVING PART OF THE WALL IN PLACE

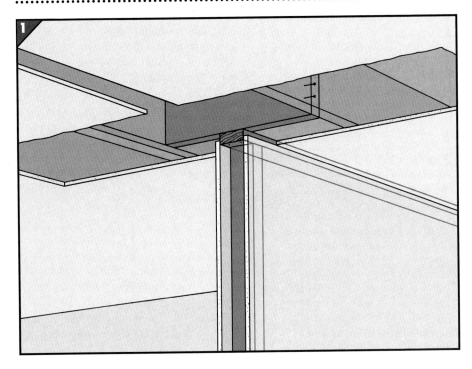

1. Securing the top plate.
◆ Designate a stud where you will stop demolition of the wall to preserve the remainder of it.
◆ Apply the methods on pages 53 to 54 to demolish the unwanted part of the wall, but cut the wall surface and plates so that they extend $1\frac{1}{2}$ inches beyond the stud designated earlier; doing so creates a pocket for the stud to be added in Step 2.
◆ Cut a hole about 1 foot wide in the ceiling, centered on the upper end of the stud and running to the second joist on either side.
◆ Nail a block of joist-dimension lumber between the joists on each side of the top plate, with the face of the block flush with the end of the plate.
◆ Nail through the plate into the edge of the block (left).

2. Reinforcing the stud.
◆ Cut a reinforcing stud to fit snugly between the top plate and soleplate, and nail it to the end stud in the section of the partition left standing (right).
◆ Surface the outer face of the reinforcing stud with wallboard and finish with corner bead (page 42).

Most homeowners can confidently remove a bearing wall up to 14 feet long. To carry the weight that was borne by the wall, a header made of laminated veneer lumber *(page 57)* is installed along the ceiling and supported by 4-by-4 posts at each end. In most cases, you can set the support posts inside the walls abutted by the header, leaving an unbroken surface when the job is done. Temporary walls erected on each side of the bearing wall shore up the ceiling until the header and posts are in place *(page 57)*.

Structural Considerations: If the load above the wall is uncommonly heavy—a concrete-floored bathroom, for example, or a bedroom containing a water bed—you may not be able to remove the wall. And before tearing down a wall that supports even an ordinary weight, you must make sure the posts that support the new header will rest on solid structure *(below)*. If you have any uncertainties at all, consult an engineer to make sure your proposed redesign adequately distributes the weight.

 TOOLS

Handsaw
Saber saw
Hammer
Level

 MATERIALS

Double-headed nails
  $(3\frac{1}{2}")$
Framing lumber (1 x 4,
  2 x 4, 4 x 4)

LVL board for header
Nails (3", $3\frac{1}{2}"$)
Wood shims

 **SAFETY TIPS**

Wear goggles to protect your eyes when hammering, sawing, and using power tools. When lifting the header into place, wear a hard hat.

A STRONG BASE FOR HEADER SUPPORTS

The posts that support a header are usually placed on the soleplate of an adjoining nonbearing wall that runs perpendicular to the wall being removed. In most cases, the plate transfers the weight to a joist directly beneath; in turn, the joist passes the weight down to a girder or bearing wall resting on the house's foundation *(right, top)*. Sometimes, however, carpenters position a soleplate between joists. In such a case, the plate and post need special blocking under them to safely transfer the weight to the girder or bearing wall *(right, bottom)*. If there is no girder or wall directly beneath, consult an architect or contractor regarding proper placement of the header posts.

To determine the nonbearing wall's location relative to the joists below, drive a nail through the floor next to the wall and find where it protrudes. If it turns out you need blocking, cut two pieces of board the width and thickness of the joists and long enough to run between the joists. Nail them together with six 3-inch nails and butt-nail them to the joists with two $3\frac{1}{2}$-inch nails for each board at each end. This blocking should fit snugly between the bottom of the subfloor and the top of the girder or wall below; shim any gaps above or below the blocking.

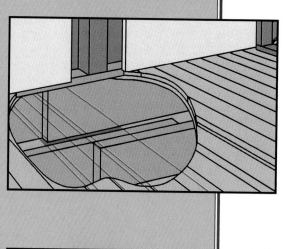

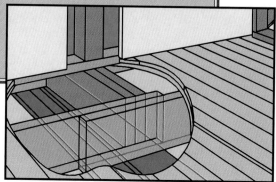

The best material to use for a new header is laminated veneer lumber, or LVL *(photograph)*. Made by gluing together thin layers of wood, LVL is lighter and stronger than ordinary lumber but just as easy to saw and nail. A coating of wax over the long edges prevents moisture from working its way between layers.

LVL is cut to order by most lumberyards; the lumberyard will also advise you on the correct width for the board. To determine the proper length, measure the distance the header must span—including the thickness of any wall surfacing—and add $3\frac{1}{2}$ inches for each end that intersects a perpendicular wall.

INSTALLING A HEADER BETWEEN WALLS

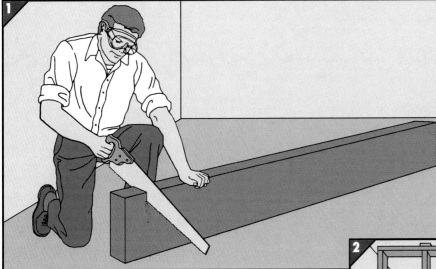

1. Preparing the header.

Cut notches into the upper corners of the header, 3 inches deep and $3\frac{1}{2}$ inches long *(left)*, so it will fit around the top plates in the adjoining walls.

2. Installing temporary supports.

Before proceeding, place the LVL header on the floor against the wall to be removed so it will be inside the workspace when the temporary walls go up.

◆ Put up stud walls about 30 inches out from the wall on both sides, following the procedure on pages 24 to 28 and using double-headed nails for easy removal later. The temporary walls should run the width of the span but need not abut a side wall closer than 2 inches.

◆ Brace the wall with a diagonal 1-by-4 nailed to every stud.

◆ Find the positions of the joists above *(page 8)* and then shim tightly between them and the top plate.

Make sure the support walls are vertical and firmly secured by their tight fit. Then remove the existing wall surface and studs in the manner shown on pages 53 to 54, Steps 1 to 3.

3. Prying out the plates.

The doubled top plates of a bearing wall are interlocked with those in the adjoining wall; use the following procedure to remove them:

◆ Cut out a 2-inch chunk of the top plates with a saber saw and begin prying a length of the doubled plate down far enough to use it as a lever. Get a firm handhold on it and work it free from its nailing in the adjoining wall.

◆ Remove the other section of the top plates in the same way.

◆ Cut and remove the soleplate as described in Step 4 on page 54.

4. Preparing the support posts.

After the wall has been removed, the breaks in the side walls will reveal pairs of close-set studs placed to provide nailing for wall surfacing *(page 54, Step 3)*.

◆ Cut the wall back to the nearest studs on either side of these nailing studs, and pry the nailing studs free *(right)*.

◆ Place the header, notched edge up, on the soleplates of the side walls at each end. Measure from the bottom of the notch to the joist above it, and cut a pair of 4-by-4 posts to this length.

◆ Test-fit the posts to make sure they provide exactly enough clearance for the notched ends of the header.

5. Raising the header.
This step will require a few helpers.

◆ Raise the header to the ceiling. Check whether it fits flush against all joists; if the center ones are low, put the header down and raise the sagging joists by tightening the shims on top of the temporary walls.

◆ While holding the header in position, insert a 4-by-4 under each end. Check the posts with a level to make sure that they are plumb.

◆ Toenail the posts to the soleplate and the header.

◆ Nail a piece of 1-by-4 about 1 foot long to each side of the header and the top of the 4-by-4 *(left)*. These boards provide a nailing surface for wallboard.

Remove the temporary walls. Patch the wall and surface the header with wallboard and corner beads *(pages 36-42).*

REMOVING PART OF A BEARING WALL

1. Positioning support studs.
When you intend to leave part of the wall intact on both sides proceed as follows:

◆ Erect temporary support walls as described in Step 2 on page 57.

◆ Dismantle the wall surface and studs back to the studs nearest the desired ends of the wall.

◆ Cut the doubled top plate flush with the stud and remove it *(page 55, Step 1).*

◆ Cut the soleplate $3\frac{1}{2}$ inches out from the studs and remove the remain-

der *(page 54, Step 4).*

◆ Use the procedure described in the box on page 56 to determine whether the existing stud stands over a joist, and install blocking if needed.

When removing one end of the bearing wall all the way to a side wall, prepare the side wall as described in Step 4 on page 58, leaving no part of the bearing wall's soleplate remaining on

that end. Notch the end of the header that will abut the side wall *(page 57, Step 1).*

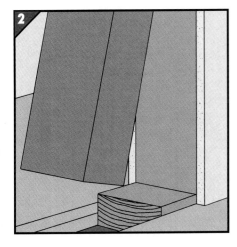

2. Raising the header.
Follow this procedure when part of the bearing wall remains intact on both sides.

◆ Place the header on the stubs of the soleplate and measure the distance from the top of the header to the joist above it. Cut two 4-by-4s to this length.

◆ Raise the header and insert the posts between it and the soleplate at both ends.

◆ At four evenly spaced points along

each post, drill counterbored holes through the post and adjacent stud, and then join the post to the stud with toggle bolts.

◆ Cover the posts and header with wallboard and corner beads.

When one end of the bearing wall is removed all the way to a side wall, cut a support post to fit into the side wall *(page 58, Step 4).* Attach the notched end of the header to that post as described in Step 5 above.

Floors and Ceilings

Creating a new living space usually involves installing or replacing a floor, a ceiling, or both. Patching an existing surface is rarely as satisfactory as putting in a new one, and some areas may not have started out with finished floors or ceilings at all. By choosing from the floor and ceiling materials in this chapter, you can make a room quieter, lighter, and better insulated and a truer reflection of your tastes.

New Floors for Basements and Attics

The areas most commonly turned into new living spaces are basements and attics. The following pages show how to lay down a smooth floor in each location.

Layered Flooring: To give floors a comfortable amount of spring, they must be built up in layers *(below)*. In an attic, the first layer consists of joists. Make sure these are the right size; a 2-by-6 joist should span no more than 8 feet, and a 2-by-8, 11 feet. If joists do not meet these guidelines, double them *(page 64)*.

On the concrete floor of a basement, boards called sleepers, made from 2-inch, pressure-treated lumber, substitute for joists. When installing sleepers over a concrete slab, it is essential first to make sure the slab is level and water resistant *(page 63)*.

 TOOLS

Hammer	Powder-actuated hammer
Metal pipe	Circular saw
Electric concrete grinder	Power screwdriver
Trowel	

 **MATERIALS**

Box nails (No. 8)	Plywood (Grade C-D $\frac{5}{8}$",
Ring-shank nails,	Grade A-C $\frac{1}{4}$",
staples, or dry-wall	tongue-in-groove)
screws *(page 65)*	Hardboard ($\frac{1}{4}$")
Cut nails ($2\frac{1}{2}$")	Roofing paper
Pressure-treated lumber	Polyethylene sheeting (6-mil)
(2 x 4s, 2 x 6s)	Flash patch compound
Standard lumber	Sandpaper (rough)
(2 x 6s, 2 x 8s)	

SAFETY TIPS

Goggles shield your eyes when you are hammering and sawing. When using power tools, protect your ears with earplugs. Wear gloves when handling pressure-treated lumber, and wash your hands thoroughly afterward.

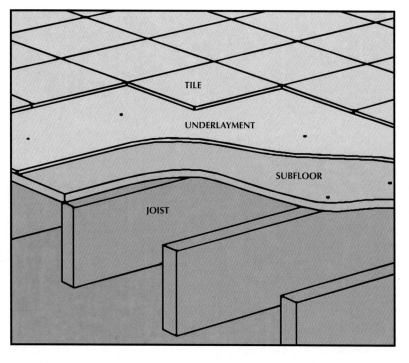

TILE

UNDERLAYMENT

SUBFLOOR

JOIST

Anatomy of a floor.

All floors share a similar structure *(left)*. At the bottom are joists or sleepers, usually spaced 16 inches apart. Nailed to these boards is a subfloor of $\frac{5}{8}$-inch-thick plywood, installed before walls are erected. Grade C-D tongue-in-groove plywood is commonly used for subflooring, with the smoother C side facing up. An additional layer, called the underlayment, provides a smooth base for the floor covering, in this case tile. Made of $\frac{1}{4}$-inch hardboard or Grade A-C tongue-in-groove plywood (C side up), the underlayment is nailed to the subfloor after walls are in place.

PREPARING A CONCRETE SLAB

1. Smoothing the slab.
◆ Check for irregularities in the slab by rolling a length of pipe over the surface while you look for slits of light under the pipe.
◆ Flatten bumps less than $\frac{1}{4}$ inch high with a rented electric concrete grinder.
◆ Fill in low areas with flash patch, a fast-drying cement-sand-epoxy compound that retains its resilience when set. Apply it with a trowel, then smooth the patches with a straightedge.

If you discover bumps more than $\frac{1}{4}$ inch high, you can create a flat surface by shimming the sleepers *(below)* that support the subfloor.

2. Dampproofing the slab.
◆ Cover the concrete with 55-pound roofing paper, available in 36-foot rolls. You need not fasten the paper to the slab; simply press it in place so that it lies flat.
◆ As additional protection against moisture, you can lay 6-mil polyethylene sheeting atop the roofing paper.

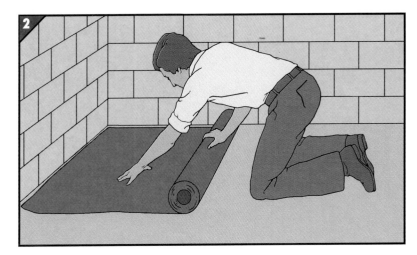

SUPPORTS FOR A SUBFLOOR

Sleepers for a slab.
Use pressure-treated 2-inch lumber for the sleepers. The boards need not all be the same width, but they must be neither warped nor twisted.
◆ Lay rows of sleepers atop the roofing paper at 16-inch intervals on center. Shim each row as necessary to compensate for low spots in the slab.
◆ Fasten the sleepers to the concrete with $2\frac{1}{2}$-inch cut nails, hammered in with a maul, or special-purpose nails driven with a powder-actuated hammer *(page 27).* Two or three nails per board are sufficient to keep the sleepers from shifting until the subfloor is in place.

PLATE

Reinforcing an attic floor.

Consult page 62 to determine whether you need to double the attic joists. If so, proceed as follows:

◆ Cut duplicate attic joists, and rest them next to the originals on the 2-by-4 plates that run the length of the attic.

◆ Using $2\frac{1}{2}$-inch nails, fasten each joist to the sides of the existing ones at several points along their lengths, and toenail the ends to the plates.

If the original joists are spaced more than 16 inches apart, install additional joists midway between them; if the original joists are doubled, double the new ones as well. Cut the new joists to the same dimensions as the originals and toenail them to the plates.

INSTALLING THE SUBFLOOR AND UNDERLAYMENT

1. Installing the subfloor.

◆ First, plan a pattern for the subfloor that avoids alignment of joints and uses as many full sheets as possible. Orient the sheets lengthwise across joists or sleepers. Leave $\frac{1}{16}$ inch between sheets where they meet end to end, and $\frac{1}{32}$ inch—the thickness of a matchbook cover—where they meet side to side.

◆ Then cut the plywood as necessary and fasten it to the sleepers or joists every 10 inches with coated No. 8 box nails.

At the ends of each plywood sheet, space the nails 6 inches apart and $\frac{3}{8}$ inch from the edges. Stagger the nails at adjoining ends to keep from splitting joists or sleepers.

◆ With the subfloor in place, check the surface for evenness.

Smooth small bumps with rough sandpaper, and fill holes with flash patch (page 63). Unusually high places may be a result of swelling of joists or sleepers; if so, pry the plywood up, trim the boards with a plane, and refasten the sheets.

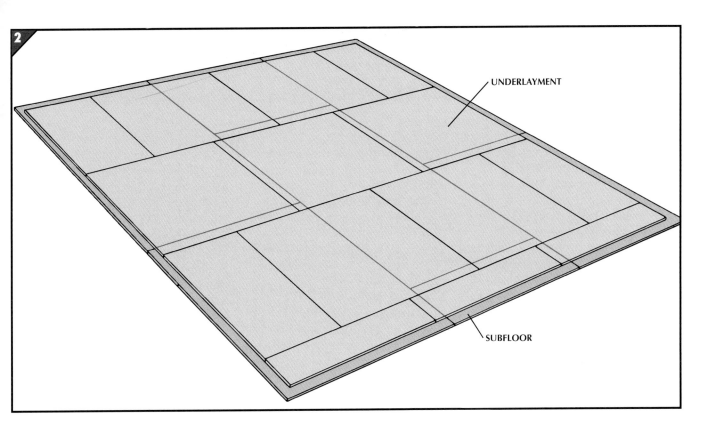

UNDERLAYMENT

SUBFLOOR

2. Installing the underlayment.

◆ After erecting walls (not shown for clarity), plan the underlayment installation so that joints between underlayment sheets do not coincide with subflooring joints *(light lines, above)*. The sheets are best laid perpendicular to those of the subfloor, and must be installed $\frac{1}{8}$ inch in from the walls, and $\frac{1}{32}$ inch from each other.

◆ Cut the plywood or hardboard sheets as necessary, and attach each one to the subfloor—not the sleepers—with the fastener of your choice *(below)*. Space the fasteners 4 inches apart over the entire sheet, and $\frac{3}{8}$ inch from the edges. To fit the last sheet in each row, follow the procedure used for border tiles, as shown on pages 68 and 69.

FOUR FASTENING METHODS

There are a number of different types of fasteners you can use for underlayment:

Coated Box Nails are covered with a film of resin that is melted by friction during driving and then rehardens to hold the nails firmly in place. The nails also have thin heads that will sink flush with the surface.

Ring-Shank Nails have ridges around the shank from top to bottom that grip the wood very tightly.

Dry-Wall Screws, driven with a screw gun, can be sunk flush with the surface of the underlayment. Although screws have the best holding power, they can be time consuming to use.

Staples must be driven by a power tool, available at tool-rental shops. Though very fast, a power stapler requires some practice, since it is easy to drive staples either too far into the surface, not far enough, or sideways.

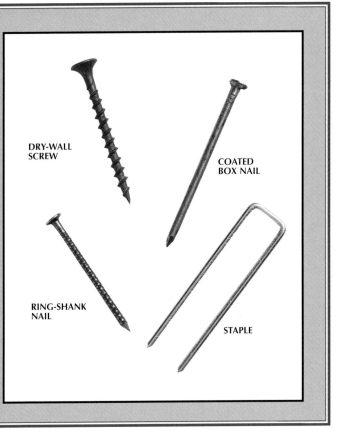

DRY-WALL SCREW

COATED BOX NAIL

RING-SHANK NAIL

STAPLE

Laying Vinyl Tiles or Parquet

Resilient vinyl tile is a popular choice of flooring for remodeled rooms. Serviceable and handsome, it is also relatively easy to install, as shown here and on pages 68 to 69. The same tile-laying system with only slight variations serves for another common variety of tile, generally known as parquet. It consists of square blocks of prefinished hardwood, sometimes with an interlocking tongue-and-groove feature *(page 70)*.

Ordering Tile and Adhesive: Write down the dimensions of the room, so that your dealer can compute the amount of tile required. Buy enough extra tile to run the length of the long wall.

Both vinyl and parquet tiles come in self-sticking versions, with adhesive on the underside beneath backing paper. However, this layer of glue is thin. You can achieve a better bond laying either these tiles or nonstick dry tiles in adhesive applied to the underlayment. Ask your dealer for the correct adhesive.

Because wood absorbs moisture, let parquet blocks stand in the room for 3 days to adjust to humidity levels before they are laid; otherwise, they may buckle after installation.

Planning the Pattern: Lay the tile in a triangular pattern over a quarter of the floor at a time; this method helps ensure straight rows and snug fits. Locate the starting point for vinyl-tile triangles in a position that avoids your having to cut narrow strips for borders *(page 67)*. In planning a parquet pattern, place whole blocks through doorways or heavy-traffic areas *(page 70);* this is necessary because glue will stand up best under constant stress if beneath a full-size block.

Because of their complex shapes, doorjambs pose special problems. As shown on page 69, there are two solutions: Either cut tiles to fit around the trim, or undercut the casing and doorstop with a special saw, allowing tiles to slip underneath. If you choose the second option, use the saw ahead of time, before applying any adhesive, and sweep up the sawdust.

A Neat, Safe Border: In some cases, the room next to a newly finished floor has carpeting that projects into the threshold between rooms. Remove a narrow strip of padding under the edge of the carpet, then fold the carpet under itself and tack it down with carpet tacks. If the carpet does not project into the threshold—or if the adjacent flooring is resilient tile—install a metal strip called a transitional threshold.

 TOOLS

Chalk line
Notched trowel
Utility knife

Mallet
Saw (10 to 14 points per inch)

 MATERIALS

Vinyl tiles
Tile adhesive
Wood blocks

Mastic
Soft wire

 **SAFETY TIPS**

Wear rubber gloves when you spread adhesive. Kneepads make any tile-laying job more comfortable.

A DRY RUN TO SET THE PATTERN

1. Lining up the tiles.
◆ Tie a chalk line between nails set near the floor in the exact middle of opposite walls of the room.
◆ Place a tile near the center of the room with its edge against the line.
◆ From this starting point, lay a row of dry tiles to the wall, making them perpendicular to the line *(right)*.
◆ If the last tile in the row leaves a space to the wall of 2 inches or more, proceed to Step 2. If there is less than a 2-inch space, move the entire row so that it is half a tile width from the wall, then move the chalk line so that it runs along the edge of the first tile in the row.

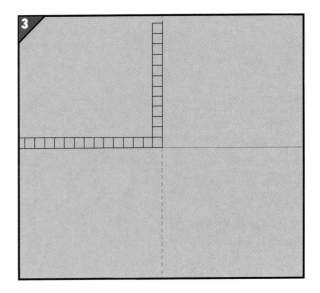

2. Marking the first line.

Press down on the chalk line in the middle of the room. Snap one side of it *(left)* and then the other so that a line of chalk is deposited.

3. A perpendicular line.

◆ Place a second row of dry tiles perpendicular to the first, with the row's edge against the chalked line *(solid line)*.
◆ If the last tile in the new row leaves a space to the wall of less than 2 inches, slide both the new row and the first row away from that wall until the last tile is

a half a tile width from the wall.
◆ Snap a second chalked line *(dashed line)* along the edge of the first row.
◆ Remove all the tiles.

If you plan to undercut the doorjamb *(box, page 69)*, do so now, before applying the adhesive and tiles.

PLACING THE TILES

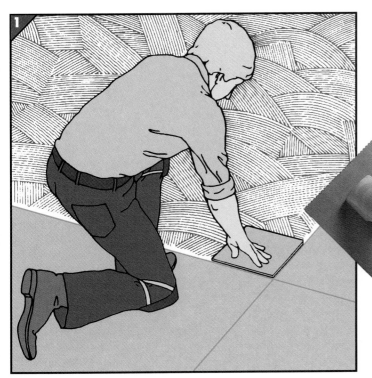

1. Starting the triangle.

◆ To lay dry tiles on an adhesive bed, spread the adhesive over a quarter of the room at a time with a notched trowel *(photograph)*, starting at the walls and working toward the room's center; do not cover the chalked lines.
◆ Begin laying tiles at the intersection of the chalked lines in the middle of the room *(left)*.

If you wish to apply adhesive-backed tiles to a dry floor, strip the backing paper off the undersides and lay the tiles directly onto the underlayment. Lay the tiles in the same way, beginning at the chalked-line intersection.

2. Setting tiles.

When laying tiles on an adhesive bed, butt each new tile against an edge of one already laid and drop the new tile in place *(right)*. Sliding it into position would force adhesive up and onto the tile's surface.

Continue the triangular pattern *(inset)* and fill as much of the remaining space as you can with whole tiles. Finish the job with partial tiles as shown below and opposite.

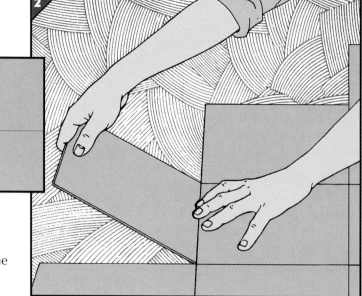

CUSTOM CUTS FOR BORDERS

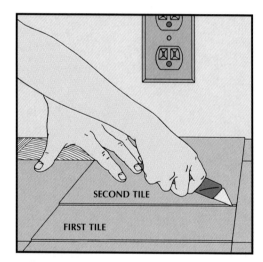

SECOND TILE

FIRST TILE

Cutting tiles for borders.
◆ Place a loose tile squarely over the fixed tile closest to the border.
◆ Hold a second loose tile over it $\frac{1}{8}$ inch from the wall.

◆ Using the second tile's edge as a guide, score the first tile with a utility knife *(left)*.
◆ Snap the scored tile. One piece will just fit into the border area.

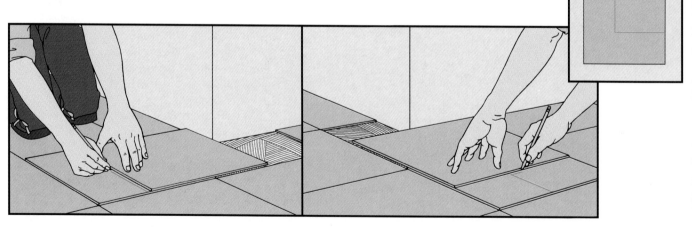

Cutting tile for corners.
◆ Place a tile squarely over the last fixed tile on the left side of the corner.
◆ Hold a second tile over the first $\frac{1}{8}$ inch from the border.
◆ Using the second tile's edge as a

guide, mark the first with a pencil *(above, left)*.
◆ Next, move the first tile, without turning it, to a position squarely over the fixed tile closest to the right side of the border *(above, right)*.

◆ Again using an overlying tile as your guide, make a second pencil line.
◆ Cut the marked tile along the pencil lines *(inset)* and fit it into the corner.

Fitting tile to irregular areas.

This is done in much the same way as shaping tiles for borders.

◆ Move the top tile along the irregular length of wall—in this case an ornate doorjamb—so that each of its corners fits successive surfaces. With each change of position, mark the underlying tile *(near right)*.

◆ If there is a curved area, bend a piece of wire—wire solder is ideal—to transfer the curve to the tile being fitted *(far right)*.

◆ Connect the various marks, cut through the tile with a utility knife, and fit it into position.

◆ Adjust if necessary by trimming with the utility knife.

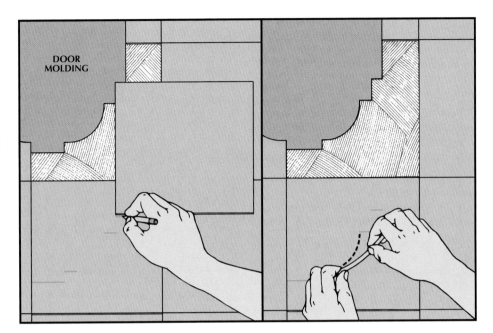

DOOR MOLDING

Cutting the Trim as Well as the Tile

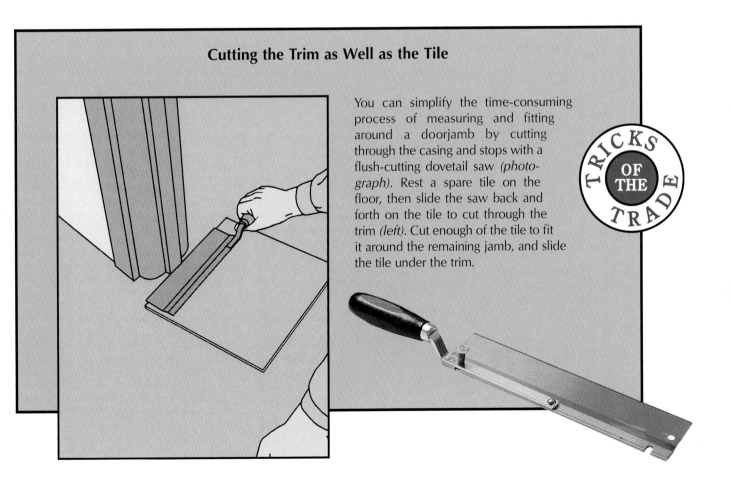

You can simplify the time-consuming process of measuring and fitting around a doorjamb by cutting through the casing and stops with a flush-cutting dovetail saw *(photograph)*. Rest a spare tile on the floor, then slide the saw back and forth on the tile to cut through the trim *(left)*. Cut enough of the tile to fit it around the remaining jamb, and slide the tile under the trim.

TRICKS OF THE TRADE

SHORTCUT TO A HARDWOOD FLOOR

1. Marking the chalked lines.

◆ Begin a row of loose blocks in the center of a doorway, with the first block set completely through the threshold.

◆ Lay blocks to the middle of the room.

◆ In the case of a room with only one door, mark a chalked line perpendicular to the row, using the edge of the last block as your guide. Lay a second row along that line. Then snap a chalked line perpendicular to the first one, alongside the edge of the first row that is closest to the center of the room.

◆ If there is another doorway in an adjoining wall, lay the second row of blocks from the center of, and through, the threshold to the middle of the room.

◆ Shift the rows so the last block in one row aligns with the last block in the other *(right)*.

◆ Snap chalked lines along one side of each row.

◆ Remove the blocks.

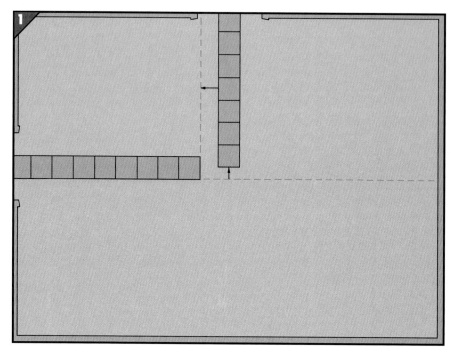

MASTIC

2. Laying the blocks.

◆ Spread a layer of mastic $\frac{1}{8}$ inch thick over a quarter of the room, using a notched trowel designed for mastic.

◆ Lay wood blocks in a triangular pattern, as described in Step 2 on page 68. With tongue-and-groove wood block, press the squares together, then place a block of wood at each edge and tap it gently with a mallet to ensure a tight fit *(left)*.

Fit blocks at borders and around doorways using the techniques described on page 69. Cut along the lines with a saw that has between 10 and 14 points per inch.

When a ceiling is added to a new living space, most people finish it with acoustical panels, acoustical tiles, or wallboard. If you wish to lower the ceiling, or if you need to cover pipes and ducts extending below the joists, a grid system of suspended panels *(below and pages 72-75)* is the best choice. If the ceiling will be left at its existing height, use either 1-foot-by-1-foot tiles or wallboard. Ceiling tiles are available in kits that provide metal strips and clips for support; alternatively, tiles can be stapled to a grid of wood furring strips nailed across joists *(pages 76-80)*. Wallboard is somewhat more difficult to install *(pages 81-83)*, but it is the least expensive ceiling material and the one most adaptable to different decorative treatments.

Lighting and Wiring: Lighting a suspended-panel ceiling is easiest with a fluorescent fixture *(pages 73-75)*. For a tile or wallboard ceiling, use a recessed lamp *(page 80)*. If you are replacing a ceiling light that was operated by a pull cord, you will need to add a wall switch *(page 75)*.

No matter what type of ceiling you plan to install, complete any extensive new wiring beforehand. Be aware that electrical connections must remain accessible when the ceiling is in place. In the case of suspended panels, all wiring above the ceiling will be readily reachable; but with tiles or wallboard, junction boxes that would be covered by the ceiling should be relocated.

⚠️ **CAUTION** *Before working with wiring, be sure the circuit is turned off at the service panel. If your house wiring is made of aluminum, have an electrician do all electrical work.*

 **TOOLS**

Tape measure
Pencil
Chalk line
Carpenter's level
Electronic stud finder
Tin snips
Utility knife
Framing square
Hammer
Pliers
String
Screwdriver
Wire cutters
Wire stripper
Staple gun
Compass
Keyhole saw
Caulking gun
Wallboard saw

 **MATERIALS**

Ring-shank dry-wall nails ($1\frac{1}{2}$")
Screw eyes
Hanger wires
Acoustical panels
Metal ceiling grid (runners and cross Ts)
Troffer light fixture
Cable connector
Electrical cable (No. 14)
Wire caps
Insulated cable staples
Black electrician's tape
Switch receptacle
Light switch
Scrap 2 x 4s
1 x 2s
Wood shims
Box nails ($1\frac{1}{2}$")
Acoustical tiles
Recessed light fixture
Common nails ($2\frac{1}{2}$", 3")
Wallboard adhesive
Wallboard

🪖 **SAFETY TIPS**

When working overhead or when nailing, protect your eyes with goggles.

A SYSTEM OF SUSPENDED PANELS

1. Measuring ceiling height.

◆ Mark the intended ceiling height on the wall at all four corners of the room. Leave a minimum of 3 inches of space below the joists, increasing the space as necessary to clear ducts, pipes, or other obstructions and also to accommodate any light fixture.
◆ Drive a nail at each corner mark.
◆ Along each wall in turn, stretch a chalk line taut between nails, check it with a level, and snap it across the wall.

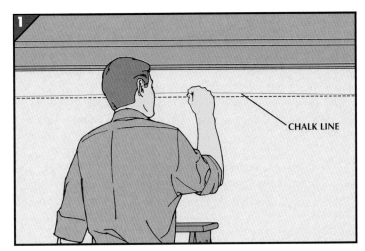

CHALK LINE

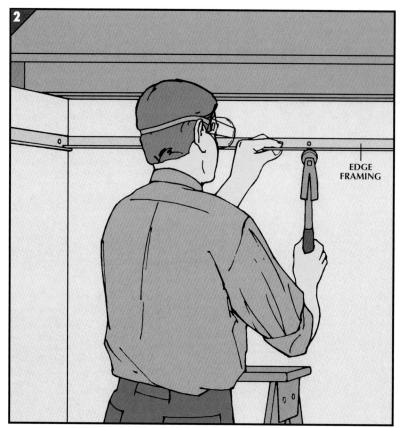

EDGE
FRAMING

2. Installing edge framing.
◆ With a stud finder, locate studs behind the walls and mark them at the chalked lines.
◆ Attach the ceiling grid's L-shaped edge framing to studs along each wall with $1\frac{1}{2}$-inch ring-shank dry-wall nails or dry-wall screws. Where the ends of two strips of framing meet at a corner, lap one end over the other. If you must cut the framing strips, use tin snips.

3. Positioning runners and cross Ts.
Runners always run perpendicular to joists; cross Ts, available in 2- or 4-foot lengths, run parallel and are supported by the runners. First, decide whether you want to install the 2- by 4-foot ceiling panels parallel or perpendicular to joists; this will determine how you measure each wall for the grid positions and what length cross Ts you must buy.

The walls that the short ends of 2- by 4-foot panels abut—shown here as walls A and B—must be divided into 2-foot intervals, centered so that edge panels will be

equal in size. Measure wall A from the midpoint to one of the corners. If the distance beyond the last 2-foot interval is 6 inches or more, mark the midpoints of walls A and B above the edge framing, then at 2-foot intervals on both sides of these marks for runners or cross Ts (right). If the distance is less than 6 inches, mark the walls a foot to one side or the other of the midpoints, then at 2-foot intervals for runners or cross Ts.

To center the long dimension of the panels, use the same method to measure walls C and D, but mark them at 4-foot instead of 2-foot intervals.

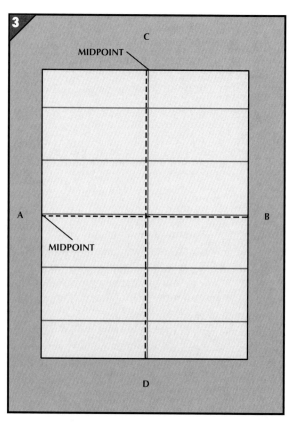

4. Attaching runners.

◆ To position the runners, snap chalked lines across the joists from the marks on the walls.

◆ Along these chalked lines, attach a screw eye to the bottom edge of every other joist. Alternatively, purchase and attach adjustable hanger wires *(photograph)*, which can be raised or lowered by turning the screw.

◆ If you are using screw eyes, insert a hanger wire in each eye, secure the wires by twisting them, and bend the free ends to 90-degree angles.

◆ To ensure alignment of the cross T slots—which occur every 6 inches in the runners—stretch a string between two of the marks for a cross T on opposite walls, and hang the runners so that a

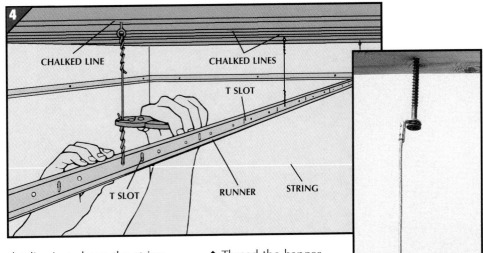

slot lies just above the string.

◆ Add lengths of runners as needed, connecting them with their end tabs. Cut off any excess with tin snips, and set each runner in place with its ends resting on the edge framing.

◆ Thread the hanger wires through the holes in the runners.

◆ Level each runner by adjusting the hanger wires, then secure each wire by twisting it around itself.

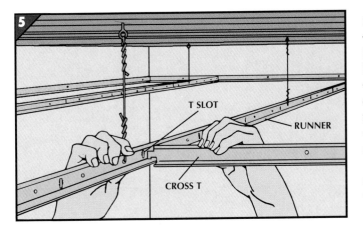

5. Connecting the cross Ts.

◆ Place cross Ts at the proper intervals and fit their ends into the slots in the runners.

◆ Along the walls, rest the outer ends of the cross Ts on the edge framing.

◆ Install panels in all the full-size openings in the grid by lifting each panel diagonally up through the framework, turning it to the horizontal,

and resting its edges on the flanges of the runners and the cross Ts. If you plan to add a light fixture *(below and pages 74-75)*, leave the grid openings surrounding the fixture empty in order to have ample room to work.

◆ With a utility knife and a framing square, trim panels to fit the smaller spaces around the walls.

ADDING A FLUORESCENT LIGHT FIXTURE

1. Connecting cable to cover plate.

◆ Knock out one of the holes in the cover plate of the light fixture and insert the threaded end of a cable connector through from the top.

◆ Attach the connector's fastener and screw it tightly in place.

◆ Cut 3 inches of sheathing off the end of a length of No. 14 plastic-

sheathed cable and then peel off $\frac{3}{4}$ inch of insulation to bare the ends of the wires.

◆ Slip the wires through the clamp on the cable connector until a little of the cable sheathing emerges from the other side.

◆ Tighten the cable clamp to secure the cable.

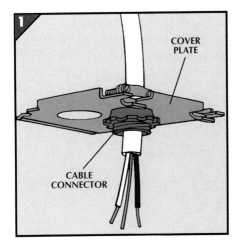

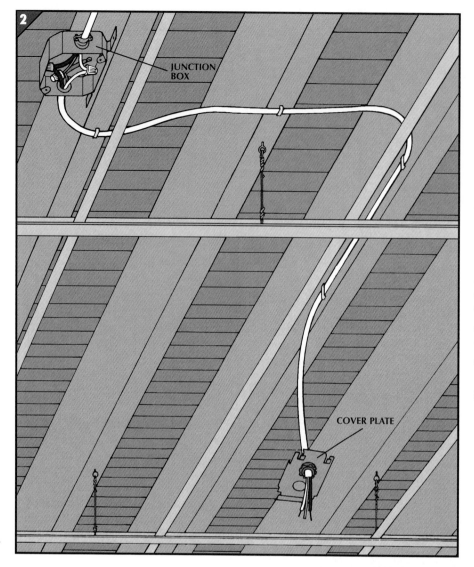

JUNCTION BOX

COVER PLATE

2. Running cable to a junction box.

◆ Turn off the electricity to the circuit at the service panel.

◆ Cut the cable long enough to reach from the planned location of the light fixture to the junction box that holds the original ceiling light.

◆ Unscrew the original fixture from the box, then disconnect and straighten the wires.

◆ Remove a knockout hole from the junction box and fasten the new cable there with another cable connector.

◆ Attach the ground wire from the cable to other ground wires and ground jumper wires in the box.

◆ With wire caps, connect the wires—white to white and black to black. Then screw a cover plate to the box.

◆ With insulated cable staples, fasten the cable to the joists to within 2 feet of the planned fixture location, but leave the plate-connected end dangling at the fixture position.

3. Putting up the fixture.

◆ Attach two screw eyes to the joist above the fixture location, loop hanger wires through them, and secure the wires by twisting them.

◆ With the help of a partner if necessary, angle the fixture into place and set it on the grid.

◆ Secure the fixture loosely to the hanger wires through the holes or loops on top of the fixture's housing.

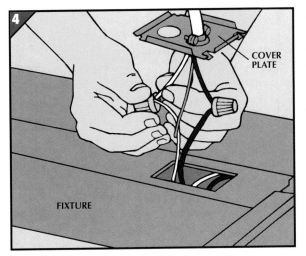

4. Connecting fixture wires.
◆ Twist together and cap the white wire from the new light fixture and the white wire of the cable, then connect the black wires.
◆ Push the wires into the opening on the fixture and then attach the cover plate.
◆ From below, open the fixture and attach the cable ground wire to a grounding screw.
◆ If the cable seems floppy, staple it at one more point near the fixture.

PROVIDING A WALL SWITCH

1. Connecting the junction box.
◆ With the electricity to the circuit still turned off at the service panel, run No. 14 cable from the planned switch location on the wall near a door to the ceiling junction box, stapling it to the joists at 4-foot intervals and at bends.
◆ Cut 3 inches of sheathing off both ends of the cable, then peel off $\frac{3}{4}$ inch of insulation to bare the wires.
◆ Run the cable through a knockout hole in the ceiling box and secure it with a clamp.
◆ Inside the box, recode the white wire from the new cable with black tape (to show that it is a hot wire in this application), twist it to the black wire from the power source, and cap the wires.
◆ Join the black wire of the new cable to the black wire from the new light fixture.
◆ Connect the white wire of the power source to the white wire of the cable from the fixture.
◆ Twist the three bare ground wires together with the green wire leading to the ground screw, then cap them.
◆ Cover the junction box with a plate.

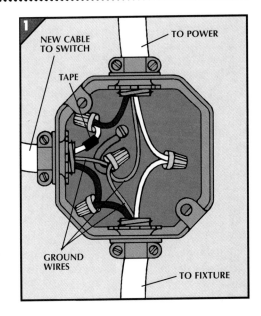

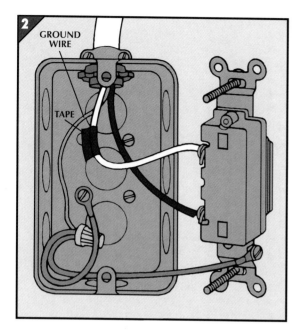

GROUND WIRE

TAPE

2. Connecting the wall switch.

◆ At the wall, install a standard outlet box *(page 28)*.

◆ Run the new cable into the box and tighten the clamp.

◆ Recode the white wire with black tape to show that it is hot, then connect the black and white wires to the terminal screws of the switch.

◆ Connect the bare ground wire of the cable with green wires leading to ground terminals on the switch and in the box.

◆ Screw the switch to the box and attach the cover plate. Turn the power back on.

AN ACOUSTICAL TILE SURFACE

1. Planning the job.

◆ At ceiling level, mark the centers of all four walls.

◆ Measure from each mark to an adjacent corner. This distance will be a number of feet plus—in most cases—a fraction of a foot. If the fraction is less than 3 inches, move the center markers 6 inches right or left.

◆ Mark 12-inch intervals from the markers to the adjoining walls.

◆ To determine how many 1-by-3 furring strips you need, count the number of interval marks on one of the walls parallel to the joists. Add two extra strips, which will be nailed next to the walls.

◆ Cut each strip the length of the walls perpendicular to the joists.

◆ To estimate the number of tiles required, count the number of 12-inch intervals on one wall, then on its adjoining wall; add one to each of these figures and multiply them.

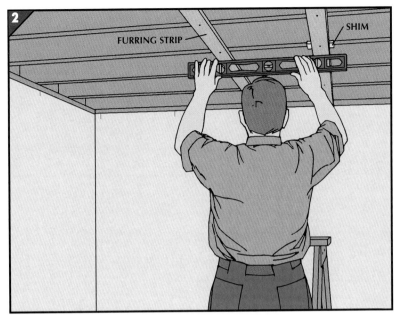

2. Putting up furring strips.

◆ Tape a carpenter's level to the narrow side of a straight 2-by-4 and check the joists lengthwise and crosswise to see how level a base they will provide. If they vary sharply, start by holding the first furring strip at right angles to the joists at their lowest level.

◆ Center the ends of the strip between the pair of marks nearest the lowest point and attach the strip to the lowest joist with a $2\frac{1}{2}$-inch nail.

◆ Using a level to guide you, shim the rest of the strip down from the higher joists.

◆ Attach the next strip between pairs of marks, leveling it from the first one *(left)*.

◆ Continue to level and nail up strips in this way, and finish by attaching furring strips to the ends of the joists against the walls.

3. Adjusting ceiling fixtures.

Any existing ceiling fixture that would interfere with a furring strip must be moved before the strip is nailed up.

◆ Turn off the electric circuit, then remove the screws or nuts holding the fixture in place and pull it away from the ceiling box.

◆ Detach the box from the joist, then reattach it to a joist so that it will be more or less in the middle of a tile, and its lower rim will be flush with the surface of the new ceiling.

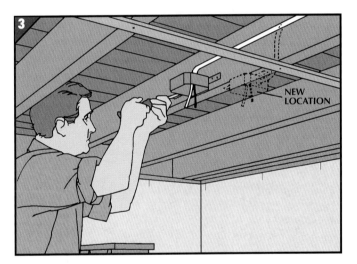

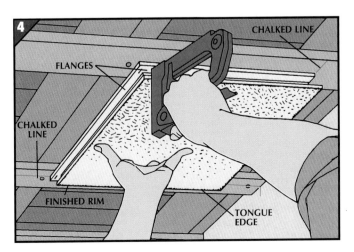

4. Putting up the first tile.

◆ Snap a chalked line down the center of the next-to-last furring strip on one side of the room.

◆ Snap another line—intersecting the first at right angles— across the room between the pair of chalk marks nearest the corner.

◆ Set the tile in the corner where the lines intersect, with the tongue edges toward the corner and the stapling flanges toward the center of the room.

◆ Align the finished rims of the tile with the chalked marks, and staple the flanges to the furring strips on both sides.

5. Attaching adjacent tiles.

◆ Slide the tongue of the next tile into the groove on the stapled edge of the preceding tile.

◆ Align the rims of the new tile with the chalked line and the rims of the preceding tile.

◆ Staple the flanges of the new tile to the furring strips.

Seating Tiles

When installing tongue-and-groove tiles, use a spare tile to fit them into place without damaging the flanges. Cut a tile in half and fit its tongue into the groove of a partially seated tile. Tap it lightly with a hammer to push the new tile into position. When the half tile becomes worn out, cut a fresh tile.

6. Adding border tiles.

◆ After installing three tiles, measure the distance from their finished rims to the walls at both ends of each tile.

◆ Deduct $\frac{1}{4}$ inch from each measurement and use the results to mark the sizes for the corner and edge tiles. Place the marks so that you will be cutting off the tongue edges rather than the flange edges.

◆ Draw lines between the marks and cut the tiles with a utility knife.

◆ Slide the pieces into place, starting with the corner tile, and anchor them to the furring strips near the wall with $1\frac{1}{2}$-inch box nails.

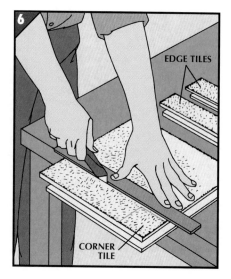

7. Marking the site of an outlet box.

◆ Tile as closely as possible to two adjacent sides of the outlet box of a ceiling fixture, then slip the tongue of a fresh tile into the groove of a tile already installed on one side of the box.

◆ Slide the loose tile up to the box and mark the tongue of the tile at the point where it touches the midpoint of the rim of the box. Do not mark the face of the tile.

◆ Slide the same tile up to the adjoining side of the box, and mark the point on the tile's other tongue where it touches the midpoint of the rim.

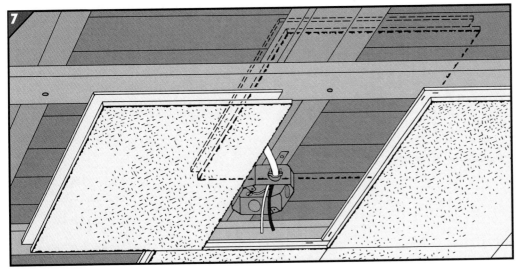

8. Cutting the hole.

◆ Using a framing square, extend the marks on the back of the tile. The point at which these lines intersect on the back of the tile marks the center of the outlet box.

◆ Transfer the center mark to the face of the tile.

◆ Set a compass to a measure that is slightly less than the size of the box.

◆ Draw a circle of this radius on the face of the tile, with the center of the circle at the point of intersection of the two lines.

◆ Using a keyhole saw held with the blade pointed outward at a slight angle, make a beveled cut around the circle through the face to the back of the tile.

◆ Staple the tile in place around the box as described on page 78, Step 5, then reattach the fixture and turn the circuit back on.

9. Finishing the ceiling.

◆ After installing all the tiles, use the procedure shown on pages 46 to 48 to miter-joint $1\frac{1}{2}$-inch cove molding to cover the junction between walls and ceiling.

◆ Attach the molding as described on pages 49 to 51.

A RECESSED LIGHT FIXTURE

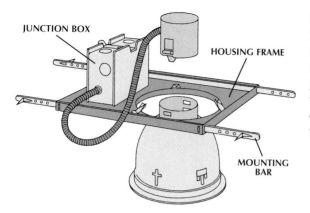

JUNCTION BOX

HOUSING FRAME

MOUNTING BAR

Selecting a fixture.

Buy a recessed fixture that is thermally protected to prevent fires. Choose one that has an attached junction box in which fixture wires can be connected to the electric cable; with this feature, you will not need to install a sep-arate outlet on the joist above the fixture. If there was a previous fixture, you can connect the new fixture to the old circuit; otherwise, extend the wiring from a nearby junction box to the desired location of the new fixture *(page 74)*.

1. Installing the housing frame.

◆ Hold in place, but do not fasten, the tile that will surround the fixture.

◆ Mark its boundaries, remove it, and position the housing frame of the fixture between the furring strips so the center of the opening in the frame will be more or less above the center of the tile.

◆ Fasten the housing frame to the edges of ad-joining furring strips by driving nails into the fur-ring strips through the holes in the mounting bars attached to two sides of the housing frame. The bottom of the housing frame should be flush with the bottom of the furring strips.

◆ Connect the fixture to a power source by join-ing the wires as described for a fluorescent fix-ture on pages 73 to 75.

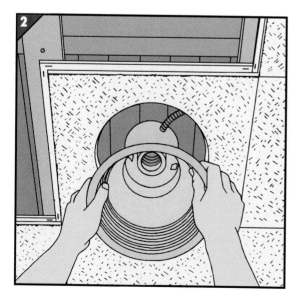

2. Completing the installation.

◆ Using the method described in Steps 7 and 8 on page 79, de-termine the location of the center of the hole you will cut in the tile to accommodate the round re-ceptacle in the bottom of the housing frame.

◆ Cut the hole and install the tile.

◆ Snap the reflector-trim unit into the socket holder, insert a bulb of the size specified by the manufacturer, and push the reflector-trim unit up into the re-ceptacle at the bottom of the housing frame.

WALLBOARD FOR THE CEILING

1. Planning a wallboard ceiling.

Measure the ceiling dimensions at the top plates of the walls, and plan to install sheets perpendicular to the joists. When you diagram the ceiling, keep in mind several principles: The ends of the wallboard must be made to land at the centers of joists—by trimming the board if necessary; these joints must be staggered to prevent a continuous seam on a single joist; and any filler strips of wallboard should be installed in the center of the ceiling. Where room dimensions create a narrow gap between the edge of a sheet and the wall, as in the L shown at right, trim back the sheet to widen the gap to at least 1 foot, and cut a piece to fill the gap.

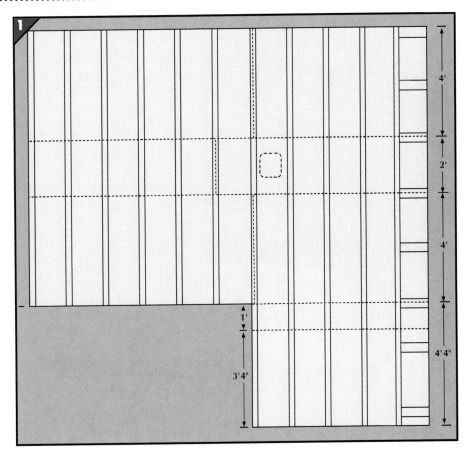

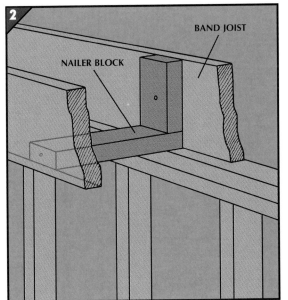

2. Providing nailing surfaces.

If the last joist lies more than 4 inches out from the wall, you must provide nailer blocks for the wallboard ends. If the joists are I-beams or open-web joists, adapt the method on page 12, Step 1, to attach the blocks to the joists.

◆ Using 2-by-4 scraps and 3-inch nails, make L-shaped nailer blocks (left) with vertical members $1\frac{1}{2}$ inches shorter than the width of the joists, and horizontal members as long as the distance between the band joist and its neighbor.

◆ Position the blocks in corners and every 24 inches in between, adjusting to provide nailing surfaces where the sheets of wallboard join.

◆ One nail will hold the upright to the band joist, another nail will secure the other end of the horizontal.

3. Marking guidelines for nails.

Make a vertical mark on the plates below the center of each joist end, and beneath the nailer blocks if you have any. The marks will establish the sight lines your wallboard nails must follow after the wallboard hides the joist itself.

4. Applying adhesive.

With a caulking gun, lay $\frac{3}{8}$-inch zigzag beads of wallboard panel adhesive along joists that will touch wallboard.

T BRACE

5. Putting up wallboard.

◆ Make a T brace the height of the ceiling and have a helper hold up the sheet while you fasten it.

◆ Place the first sheet in a corner and center its end on the joist where it will join another sheet.

◆ Secure the board with pairs of $1\frac{1}{2}$-inch ring-shank dry-wall nails or screws driven into each joist at the center of the sheet. For nails, dimple the board around each nail (page 38, Step 2).

◆ Fasten the tapered sides of the panel to each joist, 1 inch from the panel edges (left).

◆ Secure the ends with nails or screws 16 inches apart and $\frac{1}{2}$ inch from the edge.

To nail, try the position professional wallboard hangers use: Hold the hammer in front of your face, with your thumb against the handle, and hit the nails by rotating your wrist and forearm (inset).

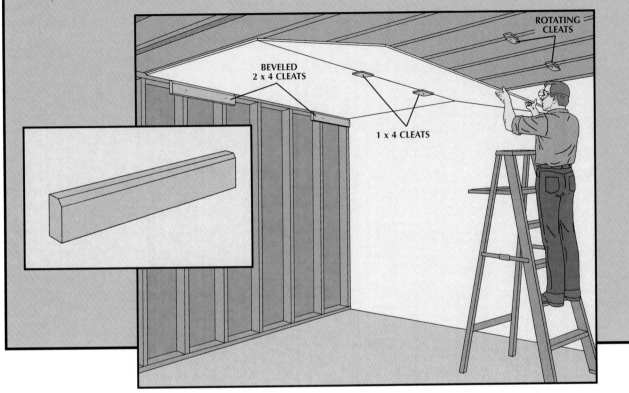

Installing a Ceiling without a Helper

If you must install a wallboard ceiling single-handedly, make a set of cleats to do the work of an assistant. Sheets next to the wall can be temporarily held in place by two 2-by-4s, beveled at the top outer edge *(inset)*, and nailed to the top plates of the wall. Subsequent sheets of dry wall can be supported by two short 1-by-4s screwed into the joists through the ad-jacent sheet, and another pair of cleats on the opposite side that can be rotated at right angles to hold the sheet when you have it in position.

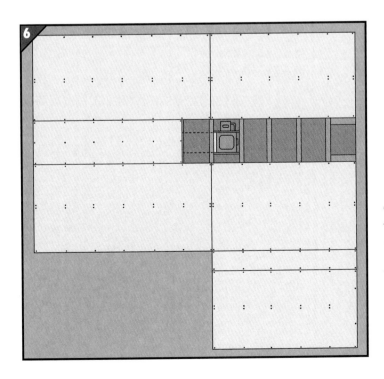

6. Nailing and fitting.

◆ To cut wallboard, score and break it as shown on page 37. Measure and cut for corners as you would for a window, in the manner shown on page 40.

◆ For lighting or ventilation openings, measure from the closest edges of mounted wallboard to the fixture or register. Use these measurements to outline the opening on the sheet, and cut it out with a wallboard saw.

◆ Fill the nail dimples and finish the joints between panels with joint compound and tape *(pages 41-42)*.

4

Creative Improvements

Making a new room out of an unfinished basement or attic, a garage, or a porch is far simpler than building an addition from scratch—the heavy work of providing a roof and a foundation has already been done. This chapter shows how to complete such transformations by adding doors and windows, supplying adequate heat, installing insulation, and applying an attractive finish to new exterior walls.

Cutting a new opening through brick veneer →

Converting a Window to a Door

Adding a new exterior door to a frame house with wood, aluminum, vinyl, or stucco siding is a fairly simple job, especially if you put it in the place of an already-existing window. The task is somewhat more laborious for a frame house covered in brick veneer but can be accomplished by adopting the methods shown on pages 96 to 99.

For easy conversion, the height and width of the window opening must match up with one of the standard sizes of prehung exterior door units. In addition, there must be no obstructions hidden in the wall beneath the window; check for pipes, cables, or ductwork, cutting a hole in the wall to carry out the inspection if necessary.

Matching the Opening: Standard prehung exterior doors—hinged on either the right or left side to open inward—are 80 inches high and 32 or 36 inches wide, not counting the jambs. To determine if the opening for an existing window can be used for such a unit, measure the window's height from the underside of the top jamb to the floor and its width between side jambs.

The Thickness Factor: For a flush fit to a frame house with conventional siding and interior walls of wallboard, choose a door unit with jambs $4\frac{5}{8}$ inches deep. If the interior walls are plaster, you need a unit $5\frac{3}{8}$ inches deep.

Unlike prehung interior doors, exterior models come only with outside trim (plus wood or metal sills). On most factory-made units, the exterior casing is 2 inches wide, extending about $1\frac{1}{2}$ inches beyond the jamb. You may want to order a unit with exterior casing that matches the size and style of existing exterior trim. Interior trim is assembled after installation, as explained on page 91.

⚠️ **CAUTION** *If you are demolishing a wall built before 1978, take all necessary precautions against the possible presence of lead paint and asbestos (page 24).*

 **TOOLS**

Hammer
Pry bar
Sledgehammer
Utility knife
Handsaw

Circular saw
Keyhole saw
Plumb line
Framing hammer
Carpenter's level
Caulking gun
Nail set

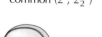 **MATERIALS**

2 x 4s
Drip flashing
Shims
Finishing nails, galvanized and common (2", $2\frac{1}{2}$")

Wood screws, aluminum ($2\frac{1}{2}$")
Adhesive caulk
Silicone caulk
Interior casing
Fiberglass insulation
Wood putty
Lockset

🪖 **SAFETY TIPS**

Protect your hands with work gloves when handling sheet metal, and add goggles and long sleeves when demolishing a wall. Goggles and earplugs are essential when using a circular saw.

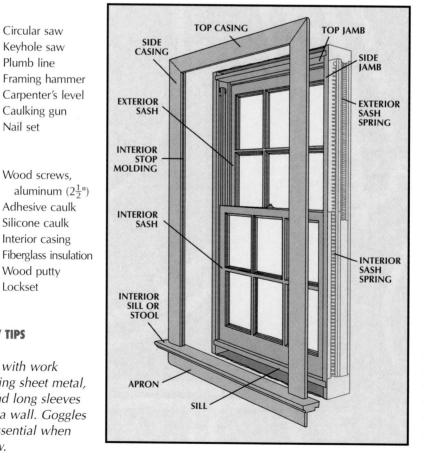

Getting at the window.
Before you can take the basic frame of a window out of a wall, you have to remove the trim and sashes piece by piece, beginning with the interior casing, the stop molding, the apron under the interior sill or stool, and the sill itself. In a standard double-hung window *(left)*, the balance mechanism that controls the two sashes is disassembled next. The type shown here consists of metal channels and springs; to remove them completely, you need to take off the exterior casing. Other mechanisms employ sash cords, metal tubes, or flexible metal tapes, and some allow the sashes to be removed from inside; a little experimenting will show you how to proceed.

1. Taking off the trim.

◆ Using a hammer and pry bar—with a block of wood placed under the bar to protect the wall—pry off the interior casing from the front of the jambs at the top and sides of the window.

◆ Remove the strips of stop molding along the side jambs (and sometimes the top jamb as well). Then pry off the apron under the sill, also known as the stool.

◆ Strike the underside of the sill with a small sledgehammer to knock it up and off the frame. Then pull out any nails protruding from the jambs and push both sashes down into the lower half of the frame.

2. Taking out the sashes.

◆ On a channel balance window *(above, left),* twist out the tops of the metal strips covering the interior sash springs, pull off the strips, and release the springs. Lift the interior sash out of the window.

◆ Working outside the house, pry off the top and side exterior casing and the stops. Free the metal strips covering the springs, release the springs, and lift out the exterior sash. Finally, remove the metal channels from the sides and top of the frame.

◆ For a double-hung window with sash cords *(above, right),* cut the two innermost cords and lift the interior sash out of the frame. The sash weights will drop behind the side jambs and can be removed when you take off the jambs.

◆ Pry off the parting strip that separates the sash channels and cut the remaining sash cords. Then lift out the exterior sash and remove the exterior casing and stops.

3. Pulling out the jambs.

Using a handsaw or a circular saw, cut the top jamb and the sill in half. Use a pry bar to loosen the top jamb and sill, and pull them out of the opening. Pry off the side jambs. Remove any nails that remain in the header, the jack studs, and rough sill.

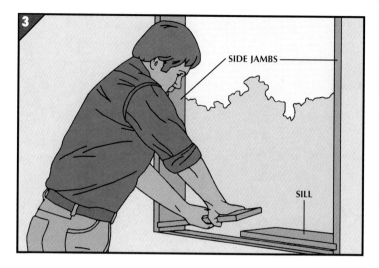

ENLARGING THE OPENING

1. Extending the interior opening.

◆ Remove the baseboard and molding from the wall below the window (page 26) and set them aside.

◆ With a keyhole saw, break through the wallboard at the rough sill at a point adjacent to one of the jack studs. Using the inner edge of the jack stud inside the wall as a guide for the saw blade, cut down from the bottom of the rough sill to the level of the soleplate (left). Repeat the procedure on the other side of the window.

◆ Using the pry bar if necessary, pry off the wallboard between the cuts to expose the framing. Pull out any insulation material inside the wall and remove any nails or drywall screws from the studs, rough sill, and soleplate.

2. Taking out the rough sill.

◆ If the rough sill is toenailed between the jack studs, saw it in two near the middle and pry off both pieces.

◆ If its ends extend under the jack studs at the sides of the rough frame, with separate jack studs between the bottom of the rough sill and the soleplate, saw the sill flush with the studs on both sides.

◆ Use a sledgehammer to knock the rough sill from the cripple stud, and pry the cripple stud off the soleplate.

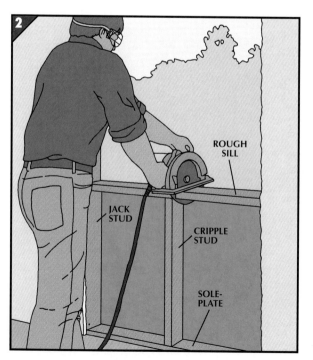

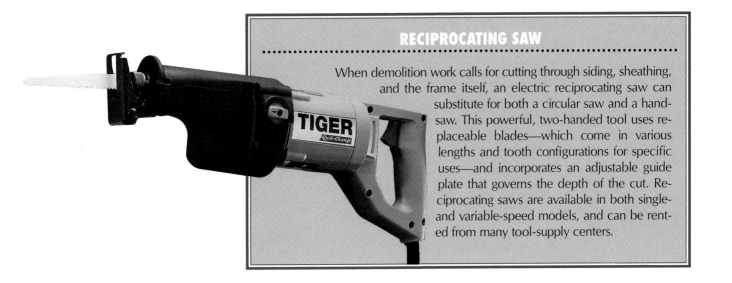

When demolition work calls for cutting through siding, sheathing, and the frame itself, an electric reciprocating saw can substitute for both a circular saw and a handsaw. This powerful, two-handed tool uses replaceable blades—which come in various lengths and tooth configurations for specific uses—and incorporates an adjustable guide plate that governs the depth of the cut. Reciprocating saws are available in both single- and variable-speed models, and can be rented from many tool-supply centers.

3. Cutting away the siding.

◆ Inside the house, measure the distance from both corners of the rough window opening to the subfloor *(page 93, Step 2)*, and transfer the measurements to the exterior siding below the rough opening.

◆ Use a carpenter's level and a straightedge to draw a horizontal line between the floor-level marks on the siding. Then draw vertical saw lines from the bottom corners of the opening in the siding down to the horizontal line.

◆ To cut through wood, aluminum, vinyl, or stucco siding, set the blade of a circular saw—a carbide-tipped blade for stucco—to the thickness of the siding; the blade should not cut into the sheathing. Cut along the lines and remove the waste siding. The border of exposed sheathing around the window opening will be extended for the door opening.

4. Extending the exterior opening.

◆ Using the level and the straightedge, mark the sheathing with two vertical saw lines from the bottom corners of the window opening to the top edge of the remaining siding.

◆ Saw through the sheathing along both lines, then saw horizontally between the bottom ends of the cuts flush with the top of the remaining siding. Remove the waste sheathing from the opening.

◆ With a handsaw, cut through the ends of the soleplate flush with the jack studs at either side of the opening. Pry the soleplate off the subfloor.

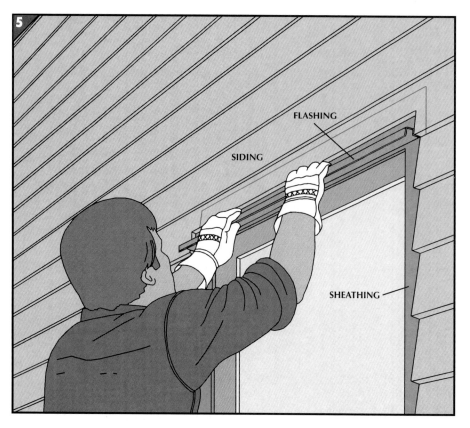

5. Putting up flashing.
◆ If there is no flashing above the opening, cut a length of preformed aluminum drip flashing to match the opening's width.
◆ Insert the flat section between the siding and sheathing and slide it up until the lower edge is flush with the top of the opening.

FITTING AND FINISHING AN EXTERIOR DOOR

1. Setting the frame in the doorway.
◆ Remove the door from the prehung door unit.
◆ Run two beads of adhesive caulk along the subfloor between the jack studs.
◆ Working from outside, set the doorframe into the opening and push it back so the outside trim rests flat against the sheathing and butts against the siding at the top and sides.
◆ Use a carpenter's level to determine whether one side of the sill is higher than the other. Drive a $2\frac{1}{2}$-inch finishing nail partway through the side jamb into the jack stud 5 or 6 inches above the higher corner.
◆ If necessary, push a wood shim under the sill near the lower corner and adjust it until the sill is level, then nail that side jamb to the jack stud.
◆ Adjust the frame in the opening, using a level to make it plumb; shim the interior edge of the top casing if necessary. Drive $2\frac{1}{2}$-inch finishing nails partway into the side jambs about a foot below the top corners.
◆ Rehang the door and shim the frame from the inside, following the directions on page 44, Step 2.
◆ Pack strips of fiberglass insulation around the top and side door jambs.

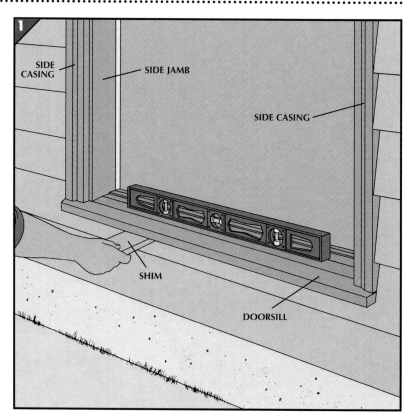

2. Finishing the exterior.

◆ Secure the top and side casings to the header and jack studs with $2\frac{1}{2}$-inch galvanized finishing nails. Nail through any shims, otherwise spacing nails at 12-inch intervals. Finish driving in the nails in the side jambs, then nail the exterior sill to the subfloor in two or three places; if the frame has an aluminum threshold, fasten it to the subfloor with $2\frac{1}{2}$-inch aluminum screws.
◆ Use a nail set to countersink the finishing nails, and fill the holes with wood putty.
◆ Pull the flashing above the doorframe down against the top casing. Finally, seal around the sides and bottom of the frame with silicone caulk.

3. Starting the interior trim.

◆ Measure how deep the barrel of the door hinge projects into the edge of the side jamb—generally between $\frac{1}{4}$ and $\frac{3}{8}$ inch. Measure the inside width of the top jamb and add the hinge-barrel depth.
◆ Mark the jamb-plus-hinge-depth measurement on the thinner edge of the interior casing and make a 45-degree outward miter cut from each mark.
◆ Center the thin edge of the casing on the face of the top jamb, at hinge-depth measurement above its lower edge, and the ends an equal distance—from $\frac{1}{8}$ to $\frac{3}{16}$ inch—beyond the inner edges of the side jambs. Nail the casing first to the jamb, then to the header above the jamb, using 2-inch finishing nails.

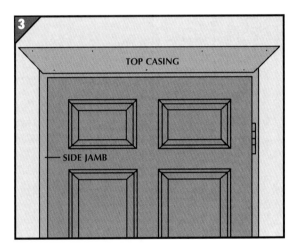

4. Finishing the interior.

◆ Saw one end of a casing strip square. Butt that end against the floor and position the strip vertically, hinge-depth distance from the inner edge of the side jamb. Mark the point where the strip meets the inner corner of the top casing and indicate the direction of the miter cut (left).
◆ Miter the casing at a 45-degree angle and set it in place. Starting at the top, use 2-inch finishing nails every 12 inches to fasten the casing to the jamb. Mark, cut, and nail the casing for the other side jamb in the same way.
◆ Measure, cut, and replace the baseboard and molding so that they abut the side casing on either side of the opening. Use a nail set to countersink all the nails in the casing, baseboard, and molding, then fill the holes with wood putty.
◆ If the door is not already fitted with door handles and a lock, install a lockset of your choice, following the manufacturer's directions.

A Window or Door Where There Was None

Whether the siding of a house is wood, aluminum, stucco, or brick, its basic structure is probably frame; that is, it has walls of wood studs and plates. You can add a new door or window opening to any frame house with the techniques shown here and on pages 96 to 98. A more complex procedure is required in houses with solid brick or concrete structural walls, which are rare today *(pages 99-102).*

Positioning the Opening: The choice of a location for the opening can involve compromises. Inside the house you may want the new window or door to fit a decorating plan or a traffic pattern; outside, it may have to align with existing openings. Before settling on placement, check for plumbing or electric lines; if lines are present, either move them or choose a new location. If you will be cutting through a brick-veneer wall, simplify the work by placing the edges of an opening along mortar lines where possible.

Special Cases: Consult a professional if you plan an opening wider than 40 inches in a brick-veneer wall or in any bearing wall *(page 52).* Even a smaller opening in a bearing wall can cause sags or cracks during construction; avoid such problems with a temporary support wall built about 2 feet inside the house *(page 57).* Shoring may also be needed for openings in an area containing a heavy steel or timber beam rather than conventional studs; get professional advice on how best to provide support.

Making the Opening: Cut through walls covered in wood, aluminum, and stucco as illustrated in the three steps at right. A brick-veneer wall calls for a slightly different procedure. For such a wall, remove the interior and mark the exterior as in Steps 1 and 2, then break through the brick and install a steel lintel *(pages 96-98);* you can buy lintels precut from a steel supplier. Complete the opening by removing any sheathing from behind the bricks as described in Step 3.

Framing Considerations: Although the temporary removal of studs within the opening will not endanger the wall structure, you must install a frame with a sturdy header as a permanent support for the wall above. Instead of the single 2-by-4 that would be used over an interior door *(pages 34-35),* you will need two pieces of 2-by-6 or larger stock, with a $\frac{1}{2}$-inch plywood filler nailed in between.

If the opening is in a nonbearing wall, the size of the stock depends on the width of the opening *(chart, below).* In a bearing wall, other factors such as the type of roof and the number of stories in the house complicate the choice of header size for even a narrow opening; consult your local building department.

 CAUTION *Before cutting through the wall, check it for asbestos and lead as explained on page 24.*

 TOOLS

Pry bar	Circular saw with
Saber saw or	masonry blade
circular saw	Cold chisel
Tin snips	Hammer drill
Plumb line	Brick set
Electric drill	Wire brush
Extended bit	Trowel
Maul	

MATERIALS

2 x 4s
Nails (2$\frac{1}{2}$", 3$\frac{1}{2}$")
Scrap plywood ($\frac{1}{2}$")
Steel lintel
Mortar
Sand

SAFETY TIPS

For demolition work, wear a dust mask, goggles, and work gloves. A long-sleeved shirt, pants, and sturdy shoes will protect against minor cuts and bruises. Replace the dust mask with a respirator when cutting through bricks with a power saw. When chiseling bricks out of the wall, wear a hard hat to protect your head from falling bricks.

HEADER SIZES FOR A NONBEARING WALL

Maximum span	Board size
3'6"	2 x 6
5'	2 x 8
6'6"	2 x 10
8'	2 x 12

Opening the interior.
Consult the chart at left to find the right board size for a header over an opening in a nonbearing wall. For most openings, 2-by-6s will do. In the case of an opening wider than 3$\frac{1}{2}$ feet— for a picture window or a patio door, perhaps—a larger header is required.

CUTTING A NEAT HOLE

1. Opening the interior.
◆ Mark the rough location of the opening, then remove full sections of baseboard and molding from the working area *(page 26, Step 4)*.
◆ With a saber saw or a circular saw set to the depth of the wall covering, cut through the plaster or wallboard from floor to ceiling just inside the studs to each side of the working area.
◆ Use a pry bar and your hands to rip away wallboard or plaster and lath inside the lines you have cut; you will need tin snips to cut away metal lath.
◆ Remove any insulation inside the wall.

2. Marking the opening.
◆ For a new door, mark the level of the top of the soleplate on the outside wall, measuring from a reference point—either a nearby door or window, or a pilot hole drilled through the wall.
◆ Mark the wall $1\frac{1}{2}$ inches lower to indicate the height of the subfloor.
◆ From the subfloor line, measure up and mark a line at the height of the doorjamb; in measuring, include the exterior casing, plus $\frac{1}{8}$ inch for clearance.
◆ Mark one side of the opening by connecting the top line and the one for the subfloor, using a plumb line or a level.
◆ Mark the top and the other side of the opening, measuring the width of the door between the outside edges of the casings and adding $\frac{1}{4}$ inch for clearance.
◆ Remove the wall covering inside the marked perimeter

(page 89, Step 3), but leave the sheathing in place.

To mark for a wood window, measure width as for a door and height from the top of the casing to the bottom of the sill, allowing $\frac{1}{4}$ inch for clearance. For a vinyl window *(page 105)*, mark the opening according to the manufacturer's instructions.

3. Cutting the sheathing.
Create an opening in the sheathing just large enough to slide the door or window jamb through, proceeding as follows:
◆ Measure the back of the top and side casing of the door or window *(inset)*.
◆ Mark and cut a hole in the sheathing that much smaller than the opening in the siding.

For a door, cut away the bottom of the sheathing all the way down to the bottom of the cut in the siding. If the opening is for a window, leave enough to fit behind the lip of the sill.

4. Preparing the interior.
◆ Inside the house, saw through the middle of any studs in the wall opening.
◆ Use a pry bar to lever them away from the remaining exterior sheathing; try not to tear the sheathing near the edges of the opening.
◆ Pull the studs away from the top plate and soleplate.

BUILDING A ROUGH FRAME

1. Erecting the frame.

Install king studs and jack studs *(page 35, Step 1)* at the left and right of the sheathing opening, using 2½-inch nails. The jack studs should stand behind the sheathing that protrudes into the exterior opening, and their tops should be even with the top of the sheathing opening.

2. Making the header.

◆ Consult the chart on page 92 for the proper board size for the header, and cut two header boards to fit horizontally between the king studs.

◆ Insert $\frac{1}{2}$-inch fillers between the header boards—scrap plywood will do—to make the header the proper thickness; nail the header together with $3\frac{1}{2}$-inch nails *(inset).*

◆ Set the header on edge on the jack studs and fasten it in place with two $3\frac{1}{2}$-inch nails driven through the king studs into the header.

◆ Fit cripple studs between the header and top plate at each point where a regular stud was removed, and toenail them in place with $2\frac{1}{2}$-inch nails.

3. Finishing the rough frame.

If the opening is for a door, complete the rough framing by cutting away the soleplate from between the insides of the jack studs.

◆ For a window opening, toenail a sill—a 2-by-4 on its side—between the jack studs just behind the bottom of the sheathing opening.

◆ Position cripple studs between the bottom of the sill and the soleplate at each point where a regular stud was removed.

◆ Drive $3\frac{1}{2}$-inch nails through the sill into the tops of the cripple studs, and toenail the bottoms of the cripple studs to the soleplate with $2\frac{1}{2}$-inch nails.

1. Scoring the brickwork.

Cutting through brick requires a circular saw outfitted with a masonry blade *(photograph)*.
◆ Open the interior of the wall, then mark the exterior opening as described in Steps 1 and 2 on page 93.
◆ Start the saw and gradually work the blade into the wall along one of the side lines of the opening.
◆ Move the saw slowly along the mark, stopping frequently to let the blade cool.

2. Cutting a lintel channel.

As you cut the channel, a few of the bricks above may tumble out.
◆ Using a cold chisel and maul—or a hammer drill—break up the mortar around the center brick in the course above the cut that marks the top of the opening. Then fracture the brick and remove the pieces.
◆ To provide shoulders for a precut steel lintel to rest on, repeat the process to open a lintel channel one brick high that extends at least one half brick beyond each side of the opening.

3. Extending the opening.

Save the bricks you remove; you will need some of them to rebrick the wall above the lintel.

Remove two courses of brick beneath the lintel channel out to the edges of the opening. To break off half a brick at the side of the opening, wedge a cold chisel, or a broad-bladed mason's chisel called a brick set, into the saw cut with its bevel facing the inside of the opening and rap it sharply with a maul.

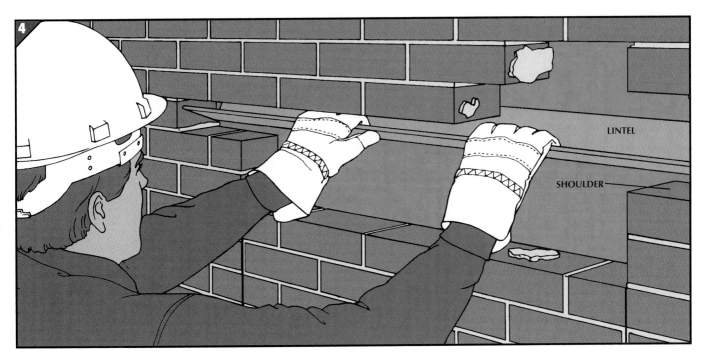

4. Setting the lintel.

◆ Chip any mortar from the shoulders of the lintel channel.
◆ Tip a steel lintel into the channel as shown above, setting the edge of the lintel flush with the face of the wall. If you find that wall ties—short lengths of metal ribbon that join the brick to the wall studding—interfere with the placement of the lintel, cut them with a cold chisel.

5. Replacing brickwork.

Use a cold chisel to remove old mortar from the bricks you reuse, and scrub them with a moistened wire brush—they should be damp but not wet. Cut bricks as explained in the box at the bottom of this page.

◆ Working from one end of the lintel to the other, apply mortar to each end and the top of a brick and slide it onto the lintel.

◆ Replace in the same manner any bricks above the opening that may have fallen. You may need to adjust the thickness of mortar joints to align these bricks with their respective courses in the wall.

6. Completing the opening.

Working from top to bottom, and from the center to the sides, remove bricks to complete the opening. Cut half bricks at the lines as described in Step 3 on page 97.

SPLITTING BRICKS
. . . .

To cut a brick crosswise, first draw a mark across it at the desired position. Then score it by tapping a brick set or cold chisel along the mark with a hammer. Place the brick on a bed of sand and break it at the mark with a sharp blow of the hammer and chisel.

Techniques for Solid Masonry

You are likely to encounter one of three types of solid masonry wall if your house is not wood framed. All can be opened for a new door or window, a process that involves many of the same techniques used for brick veneer *(pages 96-98)* but calls for some special steps that depend on how the wall is constructed.

Variations on Masonry: Some old homes have solid walls consisting of two courses of brick; such a double brick wall is opened as shown below and on page 100. Other masonry walls are made of 4-inch-thick concrete block or cinder block with a face veneer of brick; as in a solid brick wall, a $\frac{1}{2}$-inch air space is often

left between the courses. The most common type of all is a single thickness of 8-inch block, widely used for basement and garage walls. Both brick-and-block walls and solid block walls are opened by the techniques described on pages 100 to 102.

Breaking Through: To cut through any masonry wall, score the opening the same way as for veneer *(page 96)*, but do the back as well as the front. Drill at least one pilot hole to ensure that the front and back scoring registers exactly. Then break through the masonry in the same way as for brick veneer.

Lintels are required at the top of door or window openings to support

the weight of the house. For a solid brick wall, use a back-to-back pair of steel angles like the ones on pages 97 to 98. If the opening is in a brick-and-block or solid block wall, a precast concrete lintel—available from a dealer in masonry materials—is needed.

Finishing the Job: A rough wood frame makes the opening ready for a new door or window. It serves as a nailing surface, and in the case of block walls also covers ragged block cores.

 *Before proceeding, check the wall for lead paint* **CAUTION** *or asbestos as explained on page 24.*

 TOOLS

Cold chisel	Circular saw
Maul (4-lb.)	Hammer
Brick set	

MATERIALS

Steel lintels
Precast concrete lintels
Lumber (1 x 4, 1 x 8, 2 x 4)
Common nails (2", $3\frac{1}{2}$")

Cut nails (2", $2\frac{1}{2}$")
Solid-core concrete blocks (4" or 8")
Newspaper
Mortar mix

SAFETY TIPS

Wear safety goggles when hammering and a dust mask when you chip out old brick or block. A hard hat is essential when you work with unsecured heavy objects overhead. Gloves protect your hands from wet mortar.

HANDLING A BRICK WALL

1. Installing the lintels.
◆ In a wall made of two courses of brick, break out the bricks above the scored opening on both the inside and outside faces of the wall, using the techniques shown on page 96.
◆ Place two steel lintels back to back and push them onto the shoulder bricks at either side of the opening until their upright backs stand directly under the cavity between the faces.
◆ Replace bricks on top of the lintels. If the lintels increase the thickness of the wall so that the replacement bricks protrude beyond the face of it, cut the backs off the bricks using the techniques shown in the box at left.
◆ Break out the rest of the opening as shown on page 97.

2. Rough-framing the opening.

◆ Cut a piece of 2-by-4 equal to the width of the opening for a header; if a window is to be installed, cut another piece the same length for a rough sill.

◆ Cut side pieces long enough to complete either a three-sided rough doorframe or a four-sided window frame.

◆ Fasten the frame together by driving $3\frac{1}{2}$-inch nails through the header into the ends of the side pieces; in the case of a window, attach the sill to the other ends of the side pieces in the same way.

◆ Set the frame in the opening flush with the interior face of the wall.

◆ With a maul, drive $2\frac{1}{2}$-inch cut nails through the frame into the mortar joints between bricks.

FRAMING A BLOCK-WALL OPENING

SHOULDER BLOCK

SHOULDER BLOCK

1. Preparing the opening.

◆ For a block wall without brick ve-neer, measure and score the opening inside and outside as you would for a solid brick wall *(page 99)*, but allow for an outer frame by increasing the size of the opening as follows: Add $1\frac{1}{2}$ inches to the width of either a door or win-dow opening; add $\frac{3}{4}$ inch to the height of a door, $1\frac{1}{2}$ inches to the height of a window.

◆ Make a lintel channel *(pages 96-97)*.

◆ If the shoulder blocks on which the lintel is to rest remain intact, tamp newspaper tightly to the bottom of the hollow cores. Fill the cores with mortar; it need not set before the lintel is installed *(opposite, top)*. In case of broken shoulder blocks, remove the blocks completely and replace them with solid-core concrete blocks.

Proceed similarly for a brick-and-block wall, except that the dimensions of the opening should be the same as for an opening in a solid brick wall *(page 99)*; no outer frame is needed.

2. Setting the lintel.

◆ For a solid block wall, order two precast reinforced lintels that are as tall and half as thick as the blocks in your wall and as wide as the opening you have made for the channel.

◆ Mortar the shoulder blocks, the blocks to the sides of the opening, and the top of each lintel. Then—with a strong helper—lift the lintel into place.

◆ Replace any damaged blocks above the lintel.

In a brick-and-block wall, install a concrete lintel over the block, but place a steel lintel over the brick-veneer course *(pages 97-98)*. To complete an opening in this type of wall, proceed to Step 5 on page 102.

3. Attaching nailers.

In 8-inch-block walls that have core openings $\frac{3}{4}$ inch or more deep, cut 3-inch pieces of 1-by-4 or larger stock and fasten them into the cores with cut nails to fill the core space. Using these nailers to secure the outer framing, rather than nailing the framing directly to the block, is preferable because it avoids chipping the block.

4. Outer framing for 8-inch block.

◆ From 1-by-8 stock, cut a header (and a sill if you are installing a window) as wide as the opening. Since some of the board will remain exposed, select a good grade of lumber.

◆ Cut two side pieces long enough to complete a three-sided doorframe or four-sided window frame.

◆ Nail the header to the side pieces; in the case of a window, attach the sill as well.

◆ Slide the frame into the opening.

◆ Secure it with 2-inch nails into the nailer blocks attached in Step 3; in an opening with no nailers, use 2-inch cut nails to fasten the frame to the masonry at the front and back of the opening.

◆ Repair any chipped blocks with mortar.

5. Adding a rough frame.

Build a rough frame out of 2-by-4s *(page 97)*. For an opening in a block wall, slide the rough frame into the outer frame so that it is flush with the inside of the opening *(above, left)*; nail it to the outer frame with 2-inch nails. If the opening is in a brick-and-block wall, anchor the rough frame directly to the opening in the block course with 2-inch cut nails *(above, right)*.

Putting in a Window

With prefabricated window units, fitting a window into a rough opening is a simple carpentry job. Made of wood, vinyl, or vinyl- or aluminum-clad wood, these units come fully assembled, some with exterior trim already attached. A double-hung window is illustrated here, but other styles—single-hung, casement, stationary, and horizontal sliding windows, for example—are also available. Choose a style and material that blends with your existing windows.

Buying the Right Unit: For a house with siding or stucco that has walls constructed of 2-by-4s, get a window that fits the opening in height, width, and thick-ness. If the walls are thicker than the standard, such as those constructed of 2-by-6s, you will need to order jamb extensions with the window unit, or you can make them yourself *(page 104, Step 2)*. For a house with masonry walls, the window exterior will be recessed, with its inside edges flush with the interior walls.

When purchasing a wood window, be careful not to buy the type—meant for new construction—that has nailing flanges projecting from the jamb. These flanges must be tucked between the exterior siding and sheathing, making it necessary for you to remove siding all around the opening before you install the window and to replace it afterward.

 TOOLS

Carpenter's level
Hammer
Caulking gun
Miter box and backsaw
Nail set

 **MATERIALS**

Prefabricated wood window
Flashing
Felt weather stripping
Jamb extensions ($\frac{3}{4}$" stock)
Wood glue
Finishing nails ($2\frac{1}{2}$")

Wood shims
Fiberglass insulation strips
Caulk
Window stool stock
Window casing stock
Wood putty

SAFETY TIPS

When hammering, wear goggles as protection against flying nails.

A WINDOW MADE OF WOOD

Anatomy of a double-hung wood window.

The upper, exterior sash of this window slides down, and the lower, interior sash slides up in channels mounted on the side jambs. Some windows use springs and balances to keep the sashes in place, but most now have channels made of compression weather stripping, which maintains pressure on the sashes to hold them open in any position; these flexible-vinyl channels can be pushed inward toward the frame, freeing the sash and allowing it to be tilted forward for cleaning. Exterior casing—or brickmold—covers the outside edges of the top and side jambs. The exterior sill slopes outward to lead rain away from the bottom of the window.

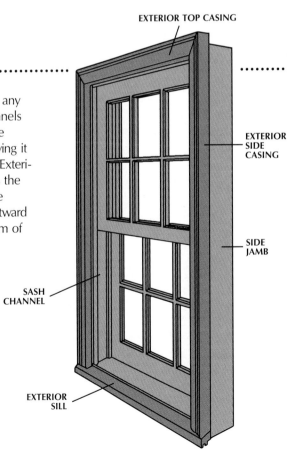

EXTERIOR TOP CASING

EXTERIOR SIDE CASING

SIDE JAMB

SASH CHANNEL

EXTERIOR SILL

FLASHING

SHEATHING

1. Tipping in the window.
◆ For a house with wood or aluminum siding or a stucco exterior, install flashing over the window opening, following the directions on page 90, Step 5.
◆ Push felt weather stripping into the gaps between the siding and the sheathing.
◆ Set the window unit in the opening, pushing it up under the flashing *(left)*, then shove the window back so the exterior casing fits firmly against the sheathing.

For a house with a masonry exterior, flashing is not necessary because the masonry will overhang the window. Set the unit in the opening and push it back to fit against the rough frame.

JAMB EXTENSION

2. Extending the jamb.
When the interior jamb of the window is not flush with the wall-finishing material you plan to use, you must make up the distance with jamb extensions.
◆ If you ordered a window with jamb extensions, use those; if not, cut $\frac{3}{4}$-inch stock into four strips of the thickness and lengths required.
◆ Glue the strips to the interior edges of the jamb and secure them with $2\frac{1}{2}$-inch finishing nails *(left)*.

3. Leveling and plumbing the window.
◆ Working outside the house, center the window between the jack studs.
◆ Lift the unit until the top jamb butts against the bottom of the header.
◆ Use a carpenter's level to determine which side of the window is lower, then nail the lower top corner to the header with a $2\frac{1}{2}$-inch finishing nail.
◆ Lower the other top corner until the window is level, and nail that corner in place.
◆ Inside the house, check the level, then wedge shims between the bottom of the window and the rough sill.
◆ Plumb the window from front to back—inserting at least two shims on each side—and fill gaps around it with strips of fiberglass insulation.
◆ Nail through all the shims into the frame.
◆ Finally, secure and caulk the exterior casing, following the directions on page 91, Step 2.

SIDE JAMB

STOOL

APRON

4. Attaching the interior stool.

◆ Finish the interior wall, butting the wall material against the window jamb.
◆ If you do not want an interior sill—called a stool—continue on to Step 5 and install casing around all four sides of the window.
◆ To make an interior stool, cut stool stock long enough to cover the front of the frame and extend on each side at least to the width of the casing you plan to use.
◆ Notch the back of the stool at both ends so the center section will fit between the side jambs. If you wish to round off the outer edge, use a wood file and sandpaper.
◆ Set the stool in place and anchor it to the bottom of the window frame with finishing nails.
◆ Cut casing or apron molding 1 inch shorter than the stool to cover the joint under the stool, rounding the bottom edge, if you wish.
◆ Nail the apron to the studs below the window *(left)*.

5. Adding interior casing.

◆ Measure the lengths of the side and top jambs. If you are adding casing to the bottom, rather than a stool, measure the bottom jamb also.
◆ Follow the directions on page 91, Steps 3 and 4, to miter, cut, and attach the casing.
◆ Countersink all interior trim nails with a nail set. Fill the holes with wood putty.

CASING

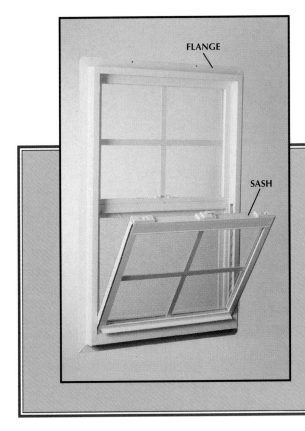

FLANGE

SASH

LOW-MAINTENANCE VINYL WINDOWS

An alternative to a wood window is one made of vinyl *(left)*, which never needs painting. As with wood windows, the single- and double-hung styles generally have tilt-out sashes for easy cleaning. Since most vinyl windows do not come with exterior casing attached, choose a type that has optional vinyl brickmold that affixes to the exterior frame. The vinyl window should have a nailing flange that attaches to the rough opening frame. Cover the flange with asphalt building paper tucked under the siding before you secure the brickmold. On the interior, add jamb extensions, stool, and casing *(Steps 2-5, opposite and above)*; or, if you will be installing wallboard *(pages 36-42)*, forgo the casing and extend the wallboard to cover the rough opening frame right up to the vinyl.

Insulation not only makes new living spaces feel comfortable but also cuts heating and cooling costs. It comes in two basic forms for unfinished walls or ceilings: blankets or batts, consisting of bundles of fiberglass or mineral fiber attached to paper or metal foil, and rigid insulating boards or panels.

Insulating Fiber: Blankets come in long rolls, batts in precut rectangles, usually 4 or 8 feet long. Both come in varying thicknesses and in $14\frac{1}{2}$-inch widths to fit between joists or studs. It is a good rule to install the thickest insulation you can fit between joists and studs without having to compress it.

Both blankets and batts can be purchased with a va-

por barrier of chemically treated or foil-lined paper that prevents the moisture-laden air of a heated room from penetrating the insulation material. Blankets and batts for use between studs and rafters usually come with stapling flanges at each side to make installation easier. Friction-fit batts, usually used between floor joists *(below)*, do not have flanges.

Thermal Panels: Rigid panels of polystyrene insulation are often used on masonry walls such as those found in basements. These 4-foot-by-$14\frac{1}{2}$-inch panels are relatively expensive but are especially efficient insulators, are easily installed between furring strips, and do not require vapor barriers.

 TOOLS

Tape measure	Hammer
Serrated knife	Saw
Staple gun	Plumb bob
Stepladder	Carpenter's level
Duct tape	

 **MATERIALS**

Insulation batts or blankets	Foam weather stripping
Insulating panels	Furring strips (1 x 2)
Scrap board (1 x 4)	Cut masonry nails (2")
Interior plywood ($\frac{1}{4}$")	Mastic adhesive
Box hinges	

 **SAFETY TIPS**

Wear long sleeves, work gloves, a face mask, and safety goggles when working with fiberglass insulation.

Insulating an attic floor.

To prevent heat loss through the floor outside a new attic room, place blankets or batts between the floor joists beyond the knee walls.

◆ Using a board to compress the material along the cutting line, trim blankets or batts to run from the wall to a point just short of the soffit vents in the eaves. These vents must be kept clear for attic ventilation.

◆ Lay the fitted blankets or batts between the joists with the vapor barrier side down.

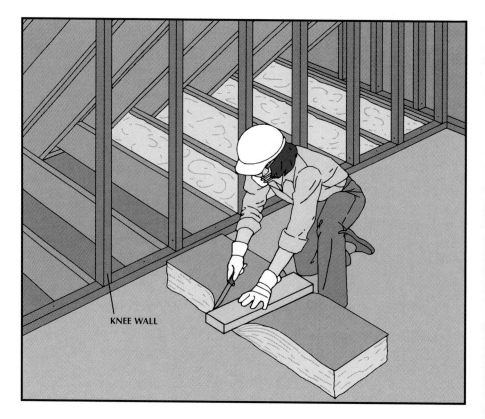

KNEE WALL

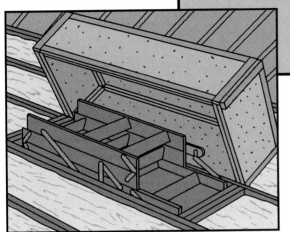

Insulating between studs and joists.

Fit insulation between studs or ceiling joists, vapor barrier side facing into the room. Staple flanges at 6-inch intervals to the inside faces of flanking studs or joists. (Stapling them to the narrow edges of the studs makes it difficult to achieve a smooth wall surface over the studs.)

In attic knee walls, fit insulation so it meets the insulation placed between joists *(opposite)*, so warm air cannot escape. Similarly, make sure insulation fits tightly without compressing it at the knee wall/stud rafter joint.

For attic ceilings, cut blankets to rafter-to-rafter measurements with about an inch extra on each end. Notch each end to fit the junction of collar beam and rafter *(page 31);* staple at 6-inch intervals to the collar beam.

Insulating between rafters.

Select a blanket or batt thickness that allows at least $\frac{1}{2}$ inch of space between the insulation and the roof sheathing, so that air can circulate freely from eave and ridgepole vents.

◆ Starting where the rafter is intersected by the ceiling collar beam, staple the blankets, vapor barrier side facing you, firmly to the inside faces of rafters at 6-inch intervals. Allow a slight overhang at the bottom to fit behind the knee wall insulation.

◆ With plastic tape or duct tape, cover the seams where the rafter insulation meets the ceiling and knee wall insulation.

Insulating a masonry wall.

◆ To make a furring grid, measure across the top and bottom of the wall and cut two 1-by-2 wood strips to this length.

◆ On the wide face of one end of a strip, mark off a box $1\frac{1}{2}$ inches wide. Make similar marks at 16-inch intervals measured from the center of one mark to the center of the next, making the last mark flush with the opposite end, even if it is not a full 16 inches from the previous mark.

◆ Lay the two strips side by side and copy the markings from one to the other *(page 25)*. Nail one strip across the top of the wall, the other across the bottom, using 2-inch cut nails at 24-inch intervals.

◆ Measure the distance between the two strips and then nail 1-by-2s of this length from the top marks to the bottom marks with 2-inch cut nails, using a plumb bob in order to make sure that the strips are perfectly vertical.

◆ Cut additional 1-by-2s to make frames around windows or doors. To complete the grid, cut 1-by-2s into $14\frac{1}{2}$-inch lengths and nail them horizontally between the vertical strips, 4 feet above the bottom strip. If necessary, use a carpenter's level to check the horizontal alignment of the strips.

◆ Fit insulation panels between the vertical and horizontal furring strips, applying mastic adhesive evenly around the edges and in an X pattern across the center to secure them in place.

◆ Save any trimmed panel scraps for piecing around windows or doors.

An Independent Source of Heat

Electric baseboard heat in a new living area is convenient and doesn't require tapping into the house's main heating system. Some units come with plugs, but most are meant to be wired directly into the house's electrical supply. For maximum comfort, place heaters on exterior walls.

A New Circuit: Whether a plug-in or hard-wired model, the heating element in a baseboard unit large enough to heat a room consumes a substantial amount of electricity. For example, baseboard heaters for ordinary 120-volt household circuits come in units drawing up to 1,500 watts of power—about 12.5 amps. More powerful models drawing 2,000 watts or more may require a 240-volt circuit.

To meet such demands, plan to run a new circuit from the service panel to the room you intend to heat.

Unless you are familiar with connecting a new circuit to the service panel, leave that part of the job to a professional. In rare instances, the electrician may recommend an increase in the amount of power coming into the house and a new service panel.

Buying the Right Size: As a rule of thumb, plan to install about 10 watts of heat for every square foot of floor area. A heating supplier can fine-tune this estimate if you provide the room's dimensions and the number of windows in it. If possible, furnish the amount of insulation in the walls, floor, and ceiling, as well as the average hours of daily winter sunlight.

> ⚠️ **CAUTION** Do not connect the new circuit to the service panel until you have finished installing the heater.

 TOOLS

Electric drill with
$\frac{3}{4}$" spade bit
Screwdrivers

Wire strippers
Dry-wall saw

 **MATERIALS**

Electrical cable
Cable clamps
Wire caps
Insulated staples

INSTALLING A BASEBOARD HEATER

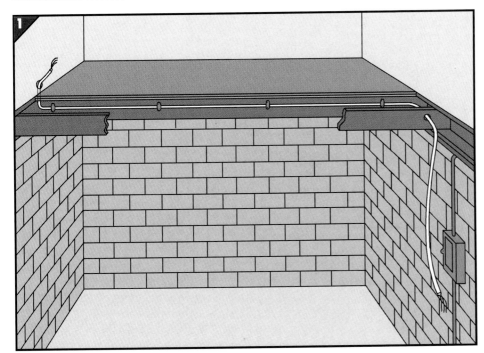

1. Running a new circuit.

◆ Baseboard heaters have a knockout toward one end, usually in the back, to accommodate electrical cable. Bore a $\frac{3}{4}$-inch hole in the wall about 2 inches above the floor where this end of the heater will be located.

◆ Route electrical cable from the service panel to the hole drilled in the wall of the new living space. Possible paths for the cable include a basement *(left),* crawlspace, or attic. Leave about 2 feet of extra cable at the service panel and at least 8 inches of cable protruding from the hole.

2. Mounting the brackets.

Lay the unit on the floor next to its planned location, remove the baseboard from the wall, and mark positions for mounting clips or screws. In one system *(right)*, clips that are screwed to the wall fit into slots in the heater back.

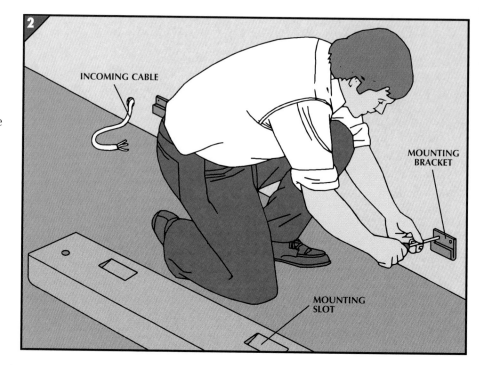

INCOMING CABLE

MOUNTING BRACKET

MOUNTING SLOT

WIRE CAPS

COVER PLATE

3. Connecting the heater.

◆ Unscrew the wiring box cover plate from the front of the heater and remove the knockout in the back of the unit.

◆ Fit the knockout hole with a cable clamp and install the cable.

◆ Strip about $\frac{3}{4}$ inch of insulation from the black and white cable wires and, using wire caps, connect these wires to the black or blue wires of the heater. When installing a 240-volt unit, mark the end of the white cable wire black, to indicate it carries current.

◆ Connect the bare ground wire in the cable to the green screw terminal in the wiring box.

◆ Replace the cover plate and complete the installation by slipping the heater onto the wall clips. If the unit has a wire for a remote thermostat, be sure that this wire remains accessible.

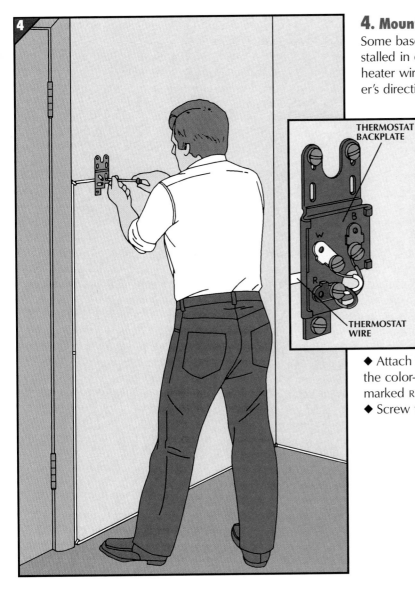

4. Mounting a remote thermostat.
Some baseboard heaters allow for a thermostat to be installed in one end of the unit. In such a case, connect the heater wires to the thermostat according to the manufacturer's directions.

THERMOSTAT BACKPLATE

THERMOSTAT WIRE

A heater that uses a separate low-voltage thermostat usually includes enough wire to install it. The manufacturer will connect this wire at the heater, but you must make the connections at the thermostat. Place the thermostat where it will not be affected by direct sunlight, drafts, or the heater itself; if possible, put it near a door so that the doorframe will partially conceal the wiring.

◆ From the heater, run the thermostat wires along baseboards, doorframes, and walls to the thermostat location, then staple them in place. If the wire is too short, replace it entirely with three-strand thermostat wire; do not use doorbell wire.

◆ Attach the thermostat backplate to the wall, then connect the color-coded thermostat wires to the backplate terminals marked R for red, B for blue and W for white *(inset)*.

◆ Screw the thermostat and its cover to the backplate.

A PLUG FOR PORTABILITY

Installing a receptacle.
Plug-in heaters come equipped with several feet of power cord; if the cord is too short to reach the nearest outlet box replace it with a longer heavy-duty cord containing No. 14-gauge wire. Then, instead of running the new circuit into the heater, install an outlet box to hold a receptacle for it.
◆ Cut an opening for an outlet box designed to clip securely to wallboard. Clamp the cable to the box and mount it in the wall.

◆ Connect the black cable wire to a brass screw terminal on a grounded receptacle and the white wire to a silver terminal.
◆ Using a wire cap and two short jumper wires, connect the bare copper cable wire to the green screw terminal of the receptacle and to a grounding screw in the back of the box *(right)*.
◆ Fasten the receptacle to the outlet box and screw a cover plate over the entire assembly.

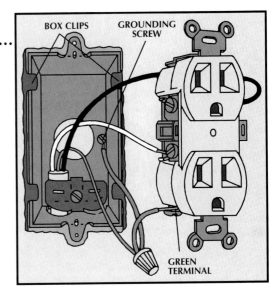

BOX CLIPS GROUNDING SCREW

GREEN TERMINAL

Turning a garage into a room is a time-honored way to gain more living space. The first step is to replace the car-entry door with a wall. You can then complete the interior with the techniques that are shown elsewhere in this book.

Taking Out the Door: Most garages have spring-powered sectional doors that roll overhead on tracks. You may want to hire a contractor to remove a door with a wind-up torsion spring, but it is possible to do it yourself *(below and at right)*. For extension springs, use the method on page 114. If the door has an electronic opener, disconnect the power and detach the mechanism before removing the spring.

Letting In Light and Air: Building codes often require window and door space equivalent to a tenth of the floor area, with at least half of that space providing ventilation openings. You can meet such requirements by framing for doors or windows in the new wall *(pages 115-116)*.

Finishing the Exterior: To complete the wall, either match the existing siding or plan for a contrasting one such as plywood *(page 117)*. You may need to break up and remove the driveway apron to align the bottom of the new siding with that beside it.

If the new siding is to lie flush with the old, select sheathing of the same thickness. Use oriented strand board—also called flakeboard—under wood shingles or vertical wood siding. Under clapboard, vinyl, aluminum, or plywood siding, install asphalt-impregnated board—pressed paper coated with tar that functions as a vapor barrier.

> ⚠️ **CAUTION** *A garage door torsion spring is under considerable tension. If you choose to remove the spring yourself, unwind it slowly, and keep your body to one side of the end of the winding rods.*

TOOLS

Hardened steel rods
Adjustable wrench
Screwdrivers
Framing hammer
Pry bar
Tape measure
Circular saw
Combination square
Carpenter's level
Powder-actuated hammer
Nail set
Caulking gun
Putty knife

MATERIALS

Standard lumber (1 x 2, 2 x 4)
Pressure-treated lumber (2 x 4)
Cut nails (2½")
Box nails (2")
Finishing nails (2½")
Common nails (2½")
Galvanized nails (2½", 2¾")
Asphalt-impregnated board
Oriented strand board
Siding
Wood lath (1")
Exterior-grade plywood (⅝")
Exterior caulking
Putty

SAFETY TIPS

Protect your eyes with goggles when removing a spring or hammering nails. Put on a dust mask when you cut pressure-treated lumber, and use work gloves to handle it. Wear ear protectors when you operate a powder-actuated hammer.

REMOVING A TORSION-SPRING DOOR

1. Loosening the setscrews.

◆ To take out a door that has a wind-up spring mechanism, obtain two cold-rolled steel rods at least 18 inches long and made for the purpose of unwinding such a spring.

◆ Lower the door to get at the spring. Then test-fit the rods in the holes in the spring's winding cone, making sure they are the right diameter and seat fully in the holes.

◆ Standing to one side of the winding cone, insert a rod in one of the holes. Apply pressure to determine the direction in which the spring will unwind.

◆ Place the other rod within easy reach.

◆ Keeping pressure on the first rod to restrain the spring, loosen the setscrews that secure the cone to the torsion shaft *(right)*.

WINDING ROD

SETSCREW

WINDING CONE

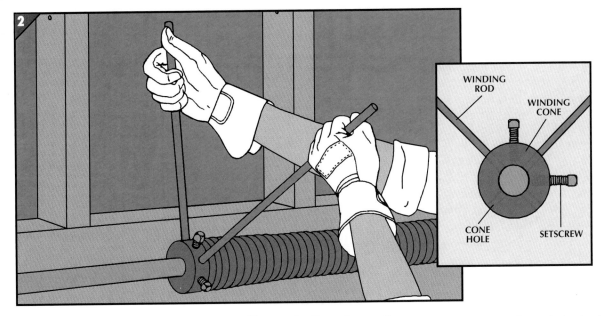

WINDING
ROD

WINDING
CONE

CONE
HOLE

SETSCREW

2. Unwinding the spring.

◆ Keeping the first rod in place, let the spring turn just enough to provide access to the next hole in the cone.

◆ Insert the second rod in the hole *(above)*.

◆ Gripping both rods near their free ends, slowly unwind the spring, alternating the rods in the holes as the cone turns *(inset)*.

◆ When the spring is unwound and the wire cable connecting it to the door hangs slack, unfasten the cable from the door.

◆ Unbolt the torsion shaft from the framing above the opening.

HEADER BEAM

DOORJAMB

GUIDE
TRACK

3. Dismantling the door.

◆ While a helper supports the top section of the door, remove the hinges and other hardware *(above)*.

◆ Lift the top section away from the one below, then remove lower sections in the same way.

◆ Starting at the rear of the garage, unbolt the horizontal sections of the two guide tracks from their overhead supports, then detach the vertical track sections from the doorjambs.

DEALING WITH EXTENSION SPRINGS

Unhooking the springs.
If your garage door employs extension springs, detach them as follows:
◆ Relax the spring tension by raising the door, then brace it open with 2-by-4s.
◆ At one side of the door, carefully remove the S hook that anchors the wire cable near the garage entrance *(right)*. Pass the hook and cable through the pulley at the end of the spring, then detach the other end of the cable from the door.
◆ Remove the cable from the other side of the door in the same way.
◆ With a helper, remove the 2-by-4 supports and lower the door; do not let it drop freely to the ground.
◆ Remove the door *(page 113, Step 3)*.

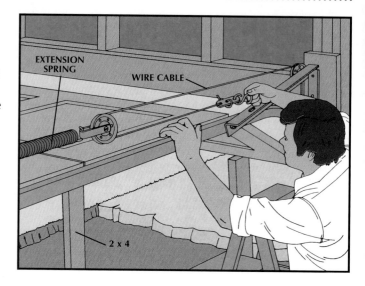

STARTING THE WALL

1. Uncovering header and studs.
With a framing hammer and pry bar, remove the jamb and trim from around the opening, leaving the existing header in place across the top; it supports the wall above the opening and distributes the weight to studs at the sides to which the new wall frame will attach.

2. Fitting the soleplate.
In most garage conversions, the new wall includes such large openings that the unsupported frame would not be rigid enough to be built separately and raised as a unit. Instead, you can construct the wall in place.
◆ Cut a piece of pressure-treated lumber to fit between the soleplates on each side of the opening; the new plate must be the same dimension as the old plate and be aligned with its outside edge.
◆ Mark the plate for 2-by-4 studs *(page 25)*, using a 16-inch spacing.
◆ Test-fit the plate *(above)*.

3. Attaching the soleplate.

◆ Try to drive a $2\frac{1}{2}$-inch cut nail through a scrap 2-by-4 and partway into the slab.

◆ If the nail holds securely and the slab does not crumble, set the new soleplate in place and nail it to the slab at 16-inch intervals, placing the nails between stud marks. Otherwise, attach the plate with a powder-actuated hammer and special fasteners.

◆ Toenail both ends of the new soleplate to the existing plates with $2\frac{1}{2}$-inch common nails *(right)*.

NEW SOLE-PLATE

TOP PLATE

JACK STUD

ROUGH SILL

SOLE-PLATE

CRIPPLE STUD

4. Constructing the wall frame.

To frame for a pair of double-hung windows spanning the full width of the opening *(above)*, proceed as follows:

◆ Cut two 2-by-4s to the width of the opening to serve as a rough sill and top plate.

◆ Nail the top plate to the existing header with $2\frac{1}{2}$-inch nails.

◆ Check the window manufacturer's instructions for the rough-opening height; measure down from the base of the top plate by this amount on each side and mark for the top of the rough sill.

◆ For each stud mark on the soleplate, cut a cripple stud to that height minus $1\frac{1}{2}$ inches.

◆ Toenail the cripple studs to the sole-plate with $2\frac{1}{2}$-inch nails. Then set the rough sill in place.

◆ Plumb each stud and secure it with two $2\frac{1}{2}$-inch nails driven through the rough sill.

◆ Cut three 2-by-4 jack studs to fit snugly between the top plate and rough sill.

◆ Nail two jack studs to the studs at either side of the opening using $2\frac{1}{2}$-inch nails at 24-inch intervals, then toenail them to the top plate and sill.

◆ Center and plumb the third jack stud between the top plate and sill, and toenail it top and bottom.

To frame smaller openings, construct a conventional stud wall *(page 25)*, rough-framing for windows or doors as shown on pages 94 to 95.

5. Attaching sheathing.

◆ Mark the centerline of each cripple stud on the outside of the slab as a nailing guide.

◆ Measure and cut sheathing to cover the frame so that any joints will be centered on the studs, allowing a gap of $\frac{1}{16}$ inch to allow for expansion. In very humid climates, leave a $\frac{1}{8}$-inch gap.

◆ Fasten the sheathing with 2-inch box nails spaced every 6 inches on the edges and every 12 inches on intermediate studs.

If you plan to match existing horizontal siding, complete Step 1 below before putting in windows or doors. Otherwise, install them at this point.

INSTALLING HORIZONTAL SIDING

STUD MARK

1. Clearing the way.

◆ On either side of the new section, remove the existing siding back to the nearest joint of each strip; if the joint is more than a few feet from the opening, remove a short section by cutting through it with a circular saw.

◆ Cut lengths of new siding to fit between the remaining strips of old siding, leaving a $\frac{1}{16}$-inch gap for expansion in the case of wood siding.

2. Attaching siding.

◆ If the bottom course of original wood siding is nailed over a starter strip, attach a lath strip at that height.

◆ Starting at the bottom, attach the new siding with galvanized nails—$2\frac{1}{2}$-inch nails for $\frac{1}{2}$-inch-thick siding, $2\frac{3}{4}$-inch nails for $\frac{3}{4}$-inch siding—according to the following patterns. Fasten bevel siding *(right)* with a nail at each stud, about an inch above the piece underneath; in the case of the lowest piece, place the nail an inch above the bottom edge. Fasten flat shiplap siding to each stud with a nail driven an inch from the top edge and another an inch from the bottom edge.

For vinyl or aluminum siding, attach the appropriate starter strip and put up the siding as shown on page 123.

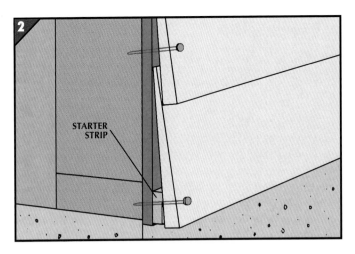

STARTER STRIP

APPLYING CONTRASTING SIDING

1. Attaching panels.

If the existing exterior is difficult to match, you can apply $\frac{5}{8}$-inch exterior-grade plywood instead.

◆ Measure and cut plywood to fit the opening in such a way that the grain of each panel's outer layer runs in the same direction and so that the joints between panels will be centered on studs with a $\frac{1}{16}$-inch gap for expansion.

◆ Apply exterior caulking to the edges, then attach the plywood with $2\frac{1}{2}$-inch galvanized nails every 16 inches along the edges of each panel and at 12-inch intervals on intermediate studs.

1 x 2

2. Trimming the new section.

◆ Apply exterior caulking along the joints between panels and wherever the plywood butts against the old siding.

◆ Cut 1-by-2 battens to attach to the plywood beside the old siding.

◆ Attach the battens with $2\frac{1}{2}$-inch finishing nails, their heads set just below the surface. Fill the nail holes with putty and caulk all joints before priming and painting.

Transforming a Porch into a Room

Enclosing a porch is easier than building an addition from scratch. Provided the original structure is sound, walling in the porch creates new living space you can heat in winter, cool in summer, and enjoy all year.

Clearing the Porch: Before you start, check local building codes and acquire a permit if you need one. Then strip the porch as described below. For a porch with partial walls, consult an engineer before proceeding; you are likely to need temporary supports for the roof.

Constructing the Floor and Walls: The next step is to lay an insulated subfloor, a task complicated by the fact that most porch floors slope to drain off rain; you can compensate with framing as shown at right and on page 120. If the existing floor is level wood with a space underneath, insulate the underside and cover the top with plywood *(page 125)*.

New exterior walls are built much like interior partitions, with only a few modifications *(page 121)*.

Completing the Job: Lightweight vinyl siding over a sheathing of asphalt-impregnated board *(page 112)* provides a simple, attractive finish for the outside walls. You can cut vinyl siding with a utility knife or tin snips, but for a big job it is faster to use a circular saw with a fine-toothed blade, reversed for a smoother cut.

Inside the new room, most of the remaining steps are familiar ones: wiring, insulating, applying wallboard, and covering the subfloor. The only unusual task may be walling over a window opening—and even that job is straightforward carpentry.

> ⚠️ **CAUTION** *Before tearing down the existing ceiling, trim, and siding, check for the presence of lead and asbestos as explained on page 24.*

 TOOLS

Pry bar
Handsaw
Circular saw
Maul (2-lb.)
Hacksaw
Tape measure

Tin snips
Level (4')
Chalk line
Caulking gun
Miter box
Backsaw
Utility knife
Heavy ruler

 MATERIALS

Common nails ($3\frac{1}{2}$")
Cut nails ($1\frac{1}{2}$", $2\frac{1}{2}$")
Galvanized roofing
  nails (1", $1\frac{1}{2}$")
Aluminum flashing
Pressure-treated
  lumber (2 x 4s)

Standard lumber
  (2 x 4s; other
  sizes as needed)
Plywood ($\frac{1}{2}$")
Wood strips ($\frac{3}{4}$")
Furring strips
  (1 x 3)
Asphalt-impregnated
  board

Foil-backed insulation batts (3" thick
  or more)
Vinyl siding and
  associated trim
Open-cell foam
Silicone-base caulk
Quarter-round
  molding

 **SAFETY TIPS**

Wear work gloves when handling pressure-treated lumber. Add goggles and a dust mask when cutting the lumber, dismantling the porch, or installing fiberglass insulation. Wear a hard hat when working with unsecured materials overhead.

Preparing the porch.

◆ Tear down the ceiling and its trim with a pry bar *(right)*.
◆ Similarly remove the frieze boards, but leave the soffits and fascias.
◆ Take out shutters, screens, screen supports, and railings.
◆ With a handsaw, cut through the doorsill along the inner edges of the side jambs to the interior subfloor. Pull the sill out. If you plan to retrim the door, pry off the exterior casings.
◆ Take out any windows *(pages 87-88)*.

Remove aluminum, vinyl, or wood siding from the wall inside the porch area with a circular saw and pry bar, making sure not to cut into the sheathing underneath. Take out rough stucco and the metal lath under it with a 2-pound maul and hacksaw. You can leave smooth stucco or other masonry in place, but add furring strips to which wallboard can later be attached.

FASCIA
SOFFIT
FRIEZE

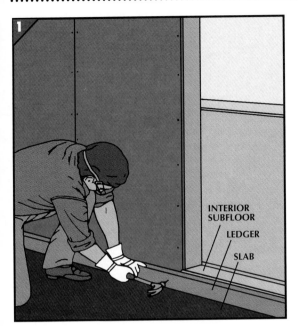

1. Attaching the ledger.

◆ Prepare the concrete slab as described on pages 62 and 63.

◆ To make the new floor flush with the interior floor, measure from the top of the interior subfloor to the slab and subtract $\frac{1}{2}$ inch.

◆ Using 2-inch pressure-treated lumber of this width, or ripped to this dimension, cut a ledger the width of the porch area.

◆ Set the ledger on the slab and attach it to the house wall with $3\frac{1}{2}$-inch common nails. For masonry walls, use $2\frac{1}{2}$-inch cut nails.

If you do not want the floors to be flush, make the ledger no smaller than a 2-by-2.

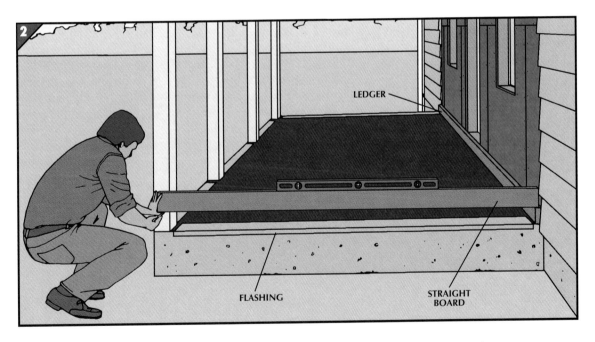

2. Putting up header joists.

◆ With tin snips, cut strips of 5-inch aluminum flashing to fit between the ledger and corner post on each side of the porch and between each pair of posts on the porch front.

◆ Lay the strips along the perimeter of the slab and fold 1 inch over the edge.

◆ Hold a straight board on edge with one end on the ledger, and place a level on the board's edge (*above*). When the board is level, mark the location of its bottom edge on the post. Do the same at each post.

◆ Cut a header joist to fit between each pair of posts by measuring from the marks to the slab and ripping a 2-inch pressure-treated board to this width.

◆ Stand each header joist on the flashing, keeping its outer edge flush with the outside edges of the posts, and toenail the board to the posts with $3\frac{1}{2}$-inch common nails.

◆ Bend the inner sections of the flashing against the inside faces of the header joists.

Labels on the upper illustration: HEADER JOIST, SLEEPER JOISTS, BAND JOIST, BRIDGES, LEDGER

3. Laying sleeper joists.

◆ Measure from the ledger to each corner post and cut 2-inch pressure-treated boards at least as wide as the header joists to make two band joists.

◆ Cut enough intermediate sleeper joists for a 16-inch spacing, measuring for each from the ledger to the header joists or front posts.

◆ Rip each joist to match the height of the ledger at one end and the header joist or post marking at the other end.

◆ Toenail joists to the ledger and posts; butt-nail to the header joists.

◆ Check the top of each joist with a level; plane off high spots and shim underneath the joist as required.

◆ Where joists are less than $2\frac{1}{2}$ inches high, secure them to the slab with cut nails. Otherwise set 2-by-4 pressure-treated bridges between the joists and nail the bridges first to the joists, then to the slab *(above)*.

◆ Bend the inner part of the side flashing against the inside face of each band joist.

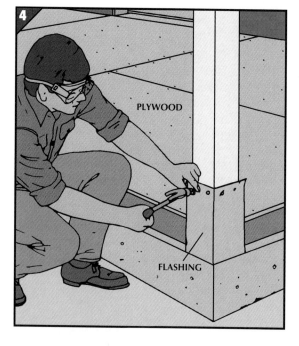

Labels on the lower illustration: PLYWOOD, FLASHING

4. Finishing the subfloor.

◆ Lay foil-backed insulation batts at least 3 inches thick between the joists, foil side up.

◆ Cover the subfloor framing with $\frac{1}{2}$-inch plywood *(pages 62-65)*.

◆ To make the bottoms of the posts watertight, set a strip of aluminum flashing 10 inches long against each post so that it extends 1 inch below the framing and its ends overlap the adjoining header joist and band joist. Secure the top of the flashing to the post with 1-inch galvanized roofing nails *(left)*.

A VINYL-CLAD EXTERIOR

1. Putting up new walls.

◆ Adapt the procedures that are shown on pages 24 to 28 and 94 to 95 to build wall frames—including window and door openings—in place, rather than assembling the frames and then raising them. Nail the top plates and soleplates to the ceiling and floor joists, respectively, then fit studs between them, doubling the end studs where the walls meet the house.

◆ To sheathe the walls, cut asphalt-impregnated board to fit from the top of each wall frame to about an inch below the lowest point of the floor joists. Butt the sheathing against door and window openings and stagger joints to avoid four adjoining corners.

◆ Attach the sheathing to the wall framing with $1\frac{1}{2}$-inch galvanized roofing nails, then install exterior doors and windows *(pages 90-91 and 103-105)*.

SHEATHING

STARTER STRIP

2. Applying the starter strips.

◆ Snap chalked lines about $1\frac{1}{2}$ inches above the bottom of the sheathing. Check at the front corners to make sure all the lines are at the same level; if not, adjust the lines until they are.

◆ Cut a starter strip *(photograph)* about 6 inches shorter than each line. If more than one piece is necessary along a side, plan for a $\frac{1}{4}$-inch gap between pieces.

◆ With a helper, align the top of the starter strip's nailing flange with the chalked line about 3 inches from the corner, letting the bottom edge extend below the sheathing.

◆ Secure the strip with $1\frac{1}{2}$-inch roofing nails at 8-inch intervals *(left)*.

⚠ **CAUTION** *Vinyl trim and siding expand and contract with heat and cold; if they are attached too securely, the finished siding will ripple. Drive nails through the centers of nailing slots and leave the heads about $\frac{1}{16}$ inch from the vinyl surface of horizontal pieces; for vertical trim, let the nailheads just touch the surface.*

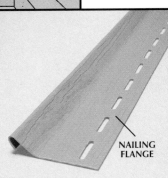

NAILING FLANGE

3. Covering an outside corner.

Next, put up an outside corner strip *(photograph)* at each front corner, as follows:

◆ Set a scrap section of siding on the starter strip and mark on the wall the position of the base of the siding.

◆ Measure from the top of the sheathing to this mark and cut an outside corner strip to that length.

◆ At a convenient height, drive a $1\frac{1}{2}$-inch galvanized roofing nail through a nailing slot on each side of the strip.

◆ Plumb the strip, then continue inserting nails on both sides at 12-inch intervals *(right)*.

◆ To prevent insects and debris from collecting inside the strip, insert open-cell foam in the top and bottom of the strip.

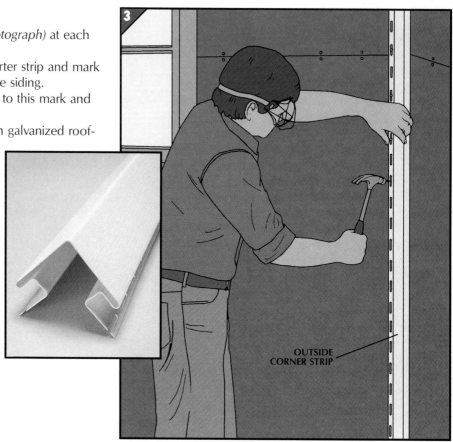

OUTSIDE
CORNER STRIP

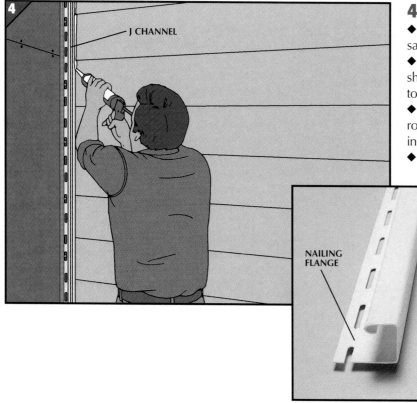

J CHANNEL

NAILING
FLANGE

4. Covering an inside corner.

◆ Cut a piece of J channel *(photograph)* the same length as the outside corner strip.

◆ Keeping the nailing flange flush with the sheathing, butt the channel as close as possible to the house wall.

◆ Plumb the strip with a level, then drive 1-inch roofing nails through the flange into the sheathing and stud behind it at 12-inch intervals.

◆ Seal the joint between the channel and the wall with silicone-base caulking compound *(left)*.

5. Completing the trim.

◆ At each window, cut undersill trim *(photograph)* to the sill length and nail it under the sill.
◆ Measure the top of the casing, add twice the width of the J channel's nailing flange to the figure, and cut a strip of J channel to that length.
◆ Add the width of the flange to the distance from the top of the casing to the base of the undersill trim. Cut two J channel strips to that length.
◆ Center the top strip above the window casing. Mark the lip at each corner of the casing.
◆ Place each side strip against the window so that the end is flush with the undersill trim's base. Mark the lip at the top corner of the casing and the top of the sill.
◆ Miter the pieces at the top-corner marks at a 45-degree angle *(page 46)*, only cutting through the lip. Below the sill mark on the side pieces cut off the raised part of the channel.
◆ Cut and bend a tab at each end of the top strip as shown in the inset.
◆ Make a corresponding notch in each side piece.
◆ Secure the three pieces with $1\frac{1}{2}$-inch roofing nails, interlocking the tabs and notches.

Cut undersill trim to fit along the top of each new wall, making it the same length as the starter strips below. With a helper, butt the lip of the trim against the soffit, level it, and nail the flange to the sheathing. If more than one piece is needed on a side, leave about $\frac{1}{4}$ inch between the strips.

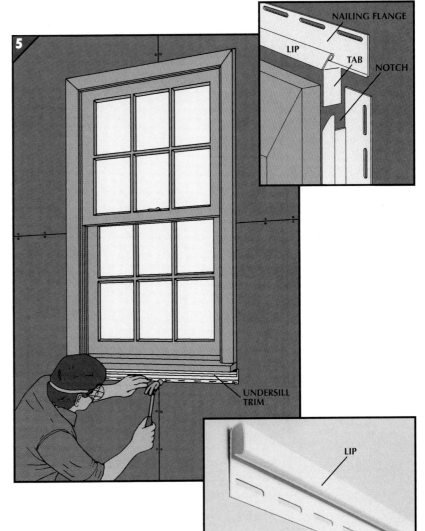

6. Attaching siding panels.

◆ Cut panels $\frac{1}{2}$ inch longer than the distance between the projecting edges of two corner strips, or of a corner strip and J channel.
◆ Fit one end of the first panel under the side trim's projecting edge, lift it to hook the lip onto the base of the starter strip, then slide the other end under the edge trim. Secure it with nails driven at 16-inch intervals.
◆ Seat and secure other panels similarly, hooking each into the groove of the preceding panel.

To join two panels end to end, allow at least 1 inch for overlap and stagger the joints from one row of panels to the next. Full-length panels come prenotched to accommodate joints; for a cut end, make a 2-inch notch yourself *(inset)*. For walls viewed primarily from one end, make sure the panel closer to the observer is the overlapping panel.

7. Fitting to openings and edges.

◆ Where a panel will meet a window or door, make two cuts from the edge of the panel to the desired depth; place the cuts for a piece fitting under the sill to allow a $\frac{1}{4}$-inch gap at each side. Score the panel lengthwise between the cuts with a utility knife.

◆ Set a heavy ruler inside the score line and bend the panel over the ruler to break off the unwanted portion.

◆ At the top of each wall, score and break off the upper edge of the top panel so that the panel extends $\frac{1}{2}$ inch under the lip of the trim. Spread clear silicone caulking under the lip of the trim, then slide in the panel.

FINISHING THE INTERIOR

Refinishing a sheathed wall.

◆ Run new circuits to the room, including one for a baseboard heater if desired *(pages 109-111)*. Insulate the walls and ceiling *(pages 106-108)*.

◆ Close off windows in the enclosed section of the old house wall by nailing 2-by-4s inside all four sides of the jamb and toenailing a 2-by-4 between the top and bottom boards. Cover the opening with sheathing *(left)*.

◆ Inside the house, adapt the methods on pages 36 to 42 to fill the window opening with a wallboard patch secured to the exposed framing. If the opening runs along stud edges, attach 1-by-2s to the studs to provide nailing surfaces.

To retrim the door, make the top and side jamb flush with the sheathing by attaching $\frac{3}{4}$-inch-wide wood strips ripped to the required thickness. Alternatively, replace the door by ripping out the jamb and installing a prehung unit *(pages 43-45)*.

Finish the ceiling and the walls with wallboard *(pages 36-42 and 81-83)*.

Adapting a masonry wall.

Provide wiring and insulation as for a sheathed wall *(opposite, bottom)*.

To hide a window recess, butt-nail 2-by-4 sleepers to the side walls of the opening, keeping the outside edges even with the masonry surface. Toenail two or more 2-by-4s between the sleepers to provide nailing surfaces for the furring strips. Inside the house, extend the cripple studs through the window opening with 2-by-4s before putting wallboard over the opening.

SLEEPER

To wallboard over all or part of the masonry wall, install 1-by-3 furring strips 16 inches apart. Attach the strips with $1\frac{1}{2}$-inch cut nails, driven into mortar joints *(above)*.

At the door, nail furring strips inside the recess to install wallboard over the masonry, then retrim the door in the new room with quarter-round molding. To replace the door, rip out the jamb but leave the rough frame *(pages 100-102)*, and install a prehung unit.

WORKING WITH A WOOD-FLOORED PORCH

Not all porches have a concrete floor. If your porch floor is made of wood, insulate it as follows, then frame, sheathe, and finish the walls as described in the preceding pages.

First, prepare the porch as described on page 118. Then saw off the edges of the floor flush with the existing support frame. If the floor joists are smaller than 2-by-8s, double them *(page 64)*.

For a floor that is level, at the desired height, and over a crawlspace, cover the ground below with sections of 6-mil polyethylene, overlapped by about 6 inches and weighted down with bricks or stones. To insulate under the porch, push 6-inch-thick batts between the joists, vapor barrier side up, and secure them with wire insulation supports *(right)*. Nail a $\frac{1}{2}$-inch plywood subfloor on top of the existing floor.

If you cannot crawl under the porch, you will need to pry up the floor planks. Lay the polyethylene through the joists onto the ground and staple insulation between the joists. Replace the planks and install the plywood.

A floor that slopes or is lower than the height desired requires an insulated wood frame covered with plywood on top of the existing porch floor. Follow the techniques for installing a subfloor over concrete *(pages 119-120, Steps 1-4)*, but use $3\frac{1}{2}$-inch nails to attach the joists.

Time-Life Books is a division of Time Life Inc.

PRESIDENT and CEO: John M. Fahey Jr.

TIME-LIFE BOOKS

MANAGING EDITOR: Roberta Conlan

Director of Design: Michael Hentges
Editorial Production Manager: Ellen Robling
Director of Operations: Eileen Bradley
Director of Photography and Research: John Conrad Weiser
Senior Editors: Russell B. Adams Jr., Janet Cave, Lee Hassig, Robert Somerville, Henry Woodhead
Library: Louise D. Forstall

PRESIDENT: John D. Hall

Vice President, Director of New Product Development: Neil Kagan
Associate Director, New Product Development: Quentin S. McAndrew
Marketing Director: James Gillespie
Vice President, Book Production: Marjann Caldwell
Production Manager: Marlene Zack
Quality Assurance Manager: James King

HOME REPAIR AND IMPROVEMENT

SERIES EDITOR: Lee Hassig
Administrative Editor: Barbara Levitt

Editorial Staff for *New Living Spaces*
Art Director: David Neal Wiseman
Picture Editor: Catherine Chase Tyson
Text Editor: Esther Ferington
Associate Editors/Research-Writing: Annette Scarpitta, Karen Sweet
Copyeditor: Judith Klein
Picture Coordinator: Paige Henke
Editorial Assistant: Amy S. Crutchfield

Special Contributors: John Drummond (illustration); Jennifer Gearhart, Marvin Shultz, Eileen Wentland (digital illustration); George Constable, Brian McGinn, Eric Weissman (text); Mel Ingber (index).

Correspondents: Christine Hinze (London), Christina Lieberman (New York), Maria Vincenza Aloisi (Paris).

PICTURE CREDITS

Cover: Photograph, Michael Latil. Art, Peter J. Malamas/Totally Incorporated.

Illustrators: Adolph E. Brotman, Nick Fasciano, Forte, Inc., Tom Gladden, Peter McGinn, John Sagan, Ray Skibinski, Vicki Vebell, Whitman Studio, Inc.

Photographers: **End papers:** Renée Comet. **9, 16, 18:** Renée Comet. **27:** Renée Comet, courtesy DESA International. **29 (2), 37, 38, 39, 51, 57, 65, 67, 69, 73, 78:** Renée Comet. **89:** Courtesy Porter-Cable Professional Power Tools. **96:** Courtesy DeWalt. **105, 121, 122, 123:** Renée Comet.

ACKNOWLEDGMENTS

Adrian Bos, Stanley Hardware, New Britain, Conn.; Arrow Group Industries, Inc., Breese, Ill.; Esther del Rosario, Washington, D.C.; Lou Genuario, Alexandria, Va.; Jeff Graboyes, The House of Doors, Alexandria, Va.; Pella Corporation, Pella, Iowa; David Stone, Styleline Division of Daston, Inc., Walworth, Wis.; Joe Teets, Falls Church, Va.

First printing. Printed in U.S.A.
Published simultaneously in Canada.
School and library distribution by Time-Life Education, P.O. Box 85026, Richmond, Virginia 23285-5026.

TIME-LIFE is a trademark of Time Warner Inc. U.S.A.

Library of Congress Cataloging-in-Publication Data
New living spaces / by the editors of Time-Life Books.
    p.   cm. — (Home repair and improvement)
Includes index.
ISBN 0-7835-3901-0
1. Dwellings—Remodeling—Amateurs' manuals.
I. Time-Life Books. II. Series.
TH4816.N475 1996
643'.7—dc20   96-152